Microcomputers
in Secondary
Education:
Issues and Techniques

Microcomputers in Secondary Education:

Issues and Techniques

Edited by J A M Howe and P M Ross,
Department of Artificial Intelligence,
University of Edinburgh

Kogan Page, London/Nichols Publishing
Company, New York

First published in 1981 by Kogan Page Ltd,
120 Pentonville Road, London N1 9JN

British Library Cataloguing in Publication Data
Microcomputers in secondary education.
    1. Computer-assisted instruction – Great Britain –
       Congresses
    2. Microprocessors – Congresses
    3. High schools – Study and teaching – Congresses
    I. Howe, J.A.M.   II. Ross, P.M.
    371.3′ 9445′ 0941   L.B. 1028.5
    ISBN 0-85038-479-6

First published in the United States of America
1981 by Nichols Publishing Company,
PO Box 96, New York, NY 10024

ISBN 0-89397-108-1

Printed in Great Britain by the Anchor Press Ltd
and bound by Wm Brendon & Son Ltd,
both of Tiptree, Essex

CONTENTS

INTRODUCTION

Besides being the first year of a new decade, 1980 was also significant because the British Government decided to respond to the microchip's arrival on the educational scene by embarking on five-year microelectronic development programmes. The objective of these programmes, being carried out separately under the auspices of the Government Education Departments for England and Wales, Scotland and Northern Ireland, is to begin to tackle the Herculean task of incorporating microelectronic technology, and micro-computers in particular, into classrooms at all levels in education.

The aim of this book is to give teachers and educators some idea of the difficulties in this, to inform them about work being carried out in classrooms and laboratories in the UK, and to offer advice to those engaged in the development of teaching software.

This is not the first government-backed foray into the use of computers in education. Between 1973 and 1978, the National Development Programme in Computer Assisted Learning promoted the use of computers for teaching and learning. However, it preceded the era of cheap computing equipment, and so not surprisingly work was largely concentrated in the higher education sector, in particular in those universities possessing expensive interactive computing facilities and staff with an enthusiasm for educational technology.

The situation has changed. Rapid developments in micro-electronic technology have been accompanied by dramatic price reductions. Now any enthusiast can purchase his own machine for a few hundred pounds and indulge in the kind of computational experiments only open, ten years ago, to those who had access to a machine costing many thousands of pounds. This has not gone unnoticed by the public at large, and many parents' associations have pre-empted their education authority by buying microcomputers, with funds raised voluntarily in their communities. We can readily envisage the time when every educational institution in the country, including primary schools and special schools, will have access to at least one microcomputer.

But what can a teacher do with a single microcomputer? This is only one of the questions tackled by the papers in this book. They record views expressed by leading authorities in the area of computer-based learning who took part in a series of symposia sponsored by the British Educational Research Association at its Annual Conference at University College, Cardiff, in 1980. The rationale for these symposia was unashamedly pedagogical. In this area, there is the ever-present danger that technological factors in the design of available hardware and available programming languages will restrict and distort educational considerations. But for these symposia, we set out to confront technology and concentrate on educational considerations, chiefly in the context of secondary education. You, the reader, may judge whether we achieved our objective.

We have decided against grouping the papers into sections. As a collection, many themes are represented, and so the ordering we chose somewhat reflects the evolution of the subject. A backcloth to the UK work is set by the early chapters by Rushby and Johnson which discuss the impact in Europe and the United States. These are followed by papers from Tagg and Fraser which discuss ways of using a single machine in the classroom for managing teaching or for providing demonstrations of hard-to-learn concepts. But many educators believe that demonstrations are not enough: children learn by doing. They envisage the time, in the not too distant future, when some schools will be equipped with clusters of machines. Instead of passively watching, pupils will have the regular use of a machine. But what form will the interaction take? Here is where we take the lid off Pandora's box. Some of the programs will only accept a restricted, stereotyped form of response, in particular those which are designed as "surrogate" teachers. Unlike in the US, these programs have never achieved popularity in the UK. As Lewis asserts, there is greater interest in using the machine as a teaching aid, to provide laboratory facilities for carrying out experiments either by using a simulation provided by a teacher or by building one's own simulation and testing it. But writing teaching software is a daunting, time-consuming task. Asking a teacher to produce a simulation program is analagous to asking, say, a physics teacher to build his own power supplies, oscilloscopes and so on, out of a basic kit of electronic parts. However, while many teachers will draw back from program building, very many enthusiasts will have a go. The papers by Lewis and by Smith and Blandford provide valuable design advice both for the novice program builder and the expert engaged in building simulations. But model building can be delegated to the pupils — this is the theme of the papers contributed

2

by du Boulay and Howe, Hart, and Howe and Ross. While model
building is a more open-ended approach than simulation, it
opens the door to many problems, especially that of guiding
the learner through a maze of concepts. This is the theme of
the final papers in the book, as contributed by Hartley,
Pask, O'Shea and Floyd, and Sharples. Every teacher brings
to the classroom his own, perhaps implicit, belief about how
children learn. He might be convinced that they learn best
by doing as they are told, or he might hold the view that
they learn best by individual effort. To some extent, these
two poles of belief are reflected in the contributions. The
earlier papers in the book, dealing with group use of the
machine are more pragmatic and appear grounded on a more
authoritarian view of education. On the other hand, the
later papers focus on individual transactions between
learner and machine; they appear to be more principled, in
the sense that the educational theory is more explicit, and
to reflect a more libertarian view. But what emerges most
clearly is the lack of an explicit theory of learning and/or
teaching which can be accepted as a basis for program design
and implementation. So building programs is largely a form
of sorcery: it is not yet a science. But in many everyday
decision making situations, we have to be satisfied with
rules-of-thumb. The reader who is interested in adding to
his existing rules will do well to consider the advice
offered on design and implementation in various papers, but
in particular in those provided by Fraser, Lewis, Smith and
Blandford, and Hartley.

The final grouping which we have identified is evaluation.
Why go to all the trouble and expense of introducing micro-
electronic technology into schools unless there is evidence
of clear benefit? This again is a bane of educationalists.
Evaluations are notoriously difficult to carry out (a)
because of the lack of good predictive educational theory,
and (b) because of the difficulty of controlling many
factors that can affect the outcome of an experiment.
Indeed, little existing classroom practice has been
evaluated formally. As Ernest Hilgard, an authority on
learning, pointed out some years ago, comparative
educational studies of such factors as class size and
teaching methods have failed to produce consistent evidence.
From his knowledge of fifty years of educational research,
he concluded that "the hopeful thing is that people gathered
together (or working alone) who want to learn, given some
learning materials, can be shown to learn". The conclusion
which follows is that we are wasting our time trying to
assess the impact of the micro-computer on learning.
Fortunately, despite formidable difficulties, a number of
investigators are still willing to try! Encouraging results,
recorded in the papers written by Johnson, du Boulay and
Howe, Hart, Hartley, and Howe and Ross, serve to whet the
appetite. If they can be built upon in the schools in years

3

to come, microelectronic technology will assume the role which earlier educational technology promised but never delivered.

JIM HOWE
PETER ROSS

Acknowledgement
We would like to record our large debt of gratitude to the Social Science Research Council of Great Britain, which has supported not only our own work but also many other projects in computing in education for a number of years. We are also extremely grateful to Gellisse Bagnall, who typed the entire manuscript into a computer, and to Jean Parker for her secretarial assistance.

MICROCOMPUTERS
IN THE CLASSROOM IN
CONTINENTAL EUROPE

Nick Rushby

Imperial College, London

1. Introduction

One, subjective, approach to this topic would be to examine
the statistical evidence about the numbers and types of
microcomputers available to schools in different European
countries. A number of interesting studies were carried out
in 1979 and 1980 from which we can discover that "microcomputers and desk top computers are usd in about 10% of
German schools" [5]; in November 1979 there were about 500
microcomputers (and about 60 minicomputers) in Swedish
schools [2]; a survey of 734 schools in England and Wales in
1980 showed that they had nearly 900 microcomputers between
them ([1], [3]).

Unfortunately, the interpretation of such figures is very
difficult and in consequence they may paint a rather
misleading picture. The number of schools with one or more
microcomputers needs to be related to the numbers and kind
of school, to the size of the school and to the utilization
of the equipment, before we can get any sort of feel for the
access which any one student may have to a microcomputer.
But is a figure which tells us that each student spends,
say, ten minutes each day working with computers, any better
guide to the impact which it may have on his education?
Perhaps not, but then this may be the only information we
have available. The other problem with such statistics is
that they are highly dependent on the sample; the schools
chosen to be included in the survey (or that choose to
include themselves by responding to the survey
questionnaire).

One criticism made of the England and Wales survey was that
it might not have reached some schools because it
represented only about 14% of the maintained secondary
schools. The figures for the numbers of microcomputers
agreed with one government estimate, but were at variance
with two other sources which indicate that there may be at
least twice as many schools (and therefore computers?)
involved [4]. Surveys are outdated very quickly,
particularly in an area where the change and growth is so
rapid. Last month's survey can grossly underestimate the

situation. Perhaps this is true for other surveys in other countries too.

It seems then that surveys are of limited use, although some may argue that, interpreted with care, they can at least give some basis for comparison - if only to show that we should always put more resources towards microcomputers in education. For this paper we will take a more subjective approach and consider how microcomputers in the classroom have been affected by political, technological and educational pressures. (This view has proved useful in the past; see [10] for a comparative study of computer based learning in continental Europe). Within each of these dimensions we can look at a number of factors which distinguish microcomputing in different countries.

Although it is true that there is some microcomputing in secondary education in every European country, we shall concentrate on those where the activity is most apparent, particularly France, the Netherlands, West Germany, Denmark and the Soviet Union, using the situation in the UK as a touchstone for comparison.

2. Applications

In those countries, as in others, we can divide the applications of microcomputers into four groups:

- administration, including such things as timetabling, word processing, stock control, school lists, sports results;

- computer studies, teaching about computers (to various degrees of detail) and their applications;

- control of other audio visual aids such as video cassette or disc players, slide projectors and, in some cases, laboratory experiments;

- learning media, computer based learning (CBL), as a different way of learning different things.

At the time of writing most of the microcomputers in all countries are used for teaching computer studies most of the time, with CBL running a close second. We shall examine the relationship between these two applications in more detail later.

As the costs of microcomputer storage fall, then the "conventional" data processing applications related to running the educational organisation will become more feasible. Until then, administrative microcomputing is

6

likely to be quantitatively less important than teaching
with and about computers.

The remaining area of application, using the microcomputer
to control a complex of learning equipment, might be
included with CBL. One of the reasons why CBL is likely to
endure (while other technologies in education have not) is
the computer's ability to control other equipment instead of
needing to be controlled. The idea of using computer based
multimedia learning (with slide projectors, audio cassette
etc) was tried in the 1960s with only limited success.

3. Political influences

In considering the political influences on the development
of microcomputers in education, it is natural to look at the
earlier initiatives in computer based learning and the
legacy they have left. During the 1970s there was a
concerted interest in CBL, with co-ordinated national
programmes to develop CBL in several European countries,
notably France [9], West Germany and the UK [6]. In other
countries, such as the Netherlands, the activity was more
fragmented [10]. The organisation of these initiatives
reflected their national attitudes to educational
organisation. Thus, in France the programme was highly
centralised [11] while in West Germany it followed the
federal structure of the central government and individual
states.

It is not surprising that the microcomputing activities a
decade later should also follow the same political
structure, reinforced perhaps by an expectation that "this
is the way things should be organised" or at least by the
experience gained in developing CBL. We can illustrate the
degree of co-ordination in each country by arranging them as
in figure 1, along a dimension with highly centralised

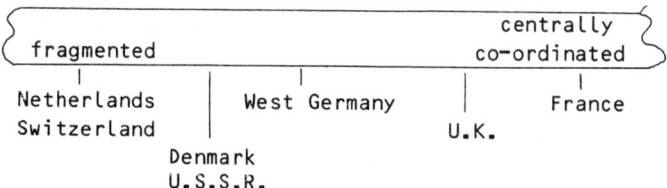

Figure 1. Coordinated or fragmented policies

policies at one end, and a fragmented approach at the other.

But, as the earlier survey by Rushby et al. [10] showed, the national programmes for developing CBL met with varied success, particularly in ensuring the long term acceptance of their aims. If the new initiatives are to succeed then we must take care to learn from the experiences – particularly from the problems and failures – of the past. There is also some indication that the pendulum has swung away from CBL applications towards computer studies. During the 1970s the emphasis and funding was directed towards learning with the aid of the computer. The new funding is accompanied by a backlash in favour of computer studies which is more discernible in some countries, for example in the UK, than in others.

4. Technological influences

There is, not surprisingly, a remarkable similarity in the microcomputer hardware throughout Europe. The microcomputers in each country range from breadboard kits for teaching logic and architecture, through small, simple microcomputers to large sophisticated systems. In that all computers need a standard set of facilities in order to function, we might agree that all microcomputers are sisters under the skin. One difference, however, is whether the microcomputers are developed specifically for educational use, as for example in Denmark (the Comet) and Austria, or whether education uses machines developed for the consumer or small business market (such as the Commodore PET and the APPLE) which are proportionally cheaper. This decision is usually influenced by political considerations and may involve pressures to support indigenous microelectronics industries.

While we can sympathise with the desire to design a micro-computer specifically for educational use, it is questionable whether the educational market in any European country is suficiently large for mass production to bring the costs of the finished machine down to compete with personal computers produced for an international consumer market. Thus far, none of the special educational micro-computers seems to have been adopted beyond its country of origin. Are we too partisan in our choice of equipment?

Turning to the programming langues used in education we find a split of opinion. In the UK, West Germany and the Netherlands, the American influence in software and in the languages available on imported American machines, has made BASIC predominant. But, both in Denmark and in France, BASIC and other similar languages have been rejected in favour of "cleaner" procedural languages designed for initial teaching, and with an eye towards their use in CBL. COMAL [8] and LSE (Language Symbolique d'Enseignement [7]) both stand in relation to BASIC as, say, PASCAL does to FORTRAN

IV; they aim to provide simplicity for beginners, together
with the constructions needed for structured programming,
and so engender good programming habits from an early age.
As we shall see later, one of the aims of LSE was that it
should be suitable for both computer studies and CBL, to
support the French philosophy of "Informatique" which
integrates the two.

Although Basic still has a strong following, particularly in
the UK and the Netherlands, its days as the dominant micro-
computer language seem numbered. Already a number of
significant and influential educational groups in North
America have turned to PASCAL (particularly UCSD PASCAL) for
their work. If previous trends of adopting North American
techniques are followed, then PASCAL will largely replace
BASIC within two or three years.

It is curious to note that BASIC is still prevalent in the
USSR despite a procedural/structured programming tradition
in that country. The reason seems to be that, until
recently, all their mini and microcomputing was carried out
on machines of North American origin, adapted to support an
extended character set. The resulting BASIC programs look
familiar, with the exception of Cyrillic characters in
remarks and in print strings. It is reasonable to suppose
that as the Soviet Union develops its own microcomputer
industry, there too education will turn away from BASIC
towards ALGOL-like languages.

5. Education influences

In all countries there is a confusion between the recent
advent of microcomputers and the use of computers in
education. Low cost microcomputing is now within the reach
of a far greater educational population and there is a
tendency to ignore the experience of the past in the belief
that the world has only just started! In turn, those whose
experience predates the 'micro revolution' have been
provoked into reactionary responses, which have been
misinterpreted as Luddite-like by the new evangelists.

There is still considerable debate as to how educational
computing fits into the curriculum alongside (or replacing?)
other subjects. Traditionally the interest in computing has
been associated with mathematics or physics and while this
may be a suitable base for some applications, it is not
clear that computer studies should be a part of the
numerical sciences. Indeed, there is a strong feeling that
such a base will discourage use by other departments in the
school.

5.1 Informatique

Further, to what extent should teaching about computers be dissociated from teaching with the aid of computers? In the UK the two applications are generally seen as distinct. Computer studies is a subject in its own right. It is accepted that we should strive to introduce this subject into the core of the curriculum so that all students will at least be "aware" of computers and their impact on society; many (perhaps most?) students should be computer literate, and the opportunities to study the subject in depth will be there for those who want to do so. On the other hand, the CBL practitioners hold that it is not necesary to be a computer specialist or programmer in order to make effective use of it as a learning medium. They make analogies with the use of educational television which does not require the teacher (or learner) to become familiar with electronics or the detailed techniques of video production. We might ask whether this distinction can, or should be, sustained in a future where personal computers in the home, workplace - and school - are commonplace? Perhaps teachers will want to understand and program these charismatic machines, and the argument that computing skills are unnecessary will then be irrelevant.

In contrast, the French approach, sometimes identified as 'Informatique', is highly integrated. From the outset of their programme to develop CBL in 58 lycees, it was decided that the participating teachers should have a thorough grounding in computer science through a one year full-time in-service training course [11]. The minicomputer systems and the programming language, LSE (mentioned above), were used both for CBL and computer studies. This philosophy has carried over to the new French programme for microelectronics in secondary education. Again, we might ask whether this integration is entirely beneficial. Perhaps there are some teachers who are discouraged from using CBL because they believe that they would not be able to master the computer studies skills - or do not care to try?

Between these two extremes of integration and separation, other European countries combine the two aspects to a greater or lesser extent as shown in figure 2. Their philosophy in this respect is a very visible characteristic of their activity.

5.2 Learning Styles

Where the computer is used as a medium for learning there are a variety of learning styles (tutorial/drill and practice, simulation and modelling, computer assisted browsing, problem solving etc). By and large, Western Europe followed the North American school of behaviourist, often

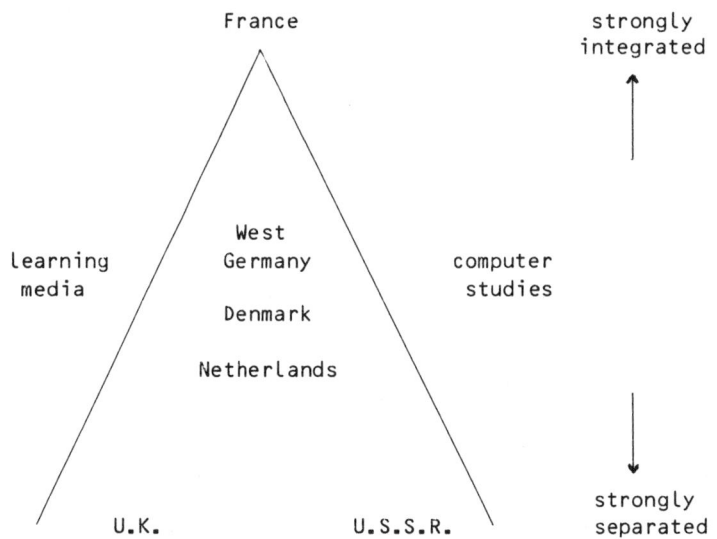

Figure 2. Integration or separation

programmed learning-like, CAL before developing other
styles. During the 1970s one could see different styles
emerging in different countries, so that the UK was noted
for its work in simulation and modelling, while the
Netherlands concentrated on tutorial modes. But, more
recently, improved communication and co-operation between
countries has spread the styles more widely so that now the
differences are less marked.

With but a few exceptions, CBL in Western Europe is
pragmatic, in that it is not firmly underpinned by learning
theory but is based on techniques that have been found to
work in practice. The lack of an educational theory of CBL
has not been considered a serious problem. After all, the
majority of teachers are not experts in learning theory but
are, nevertheless, able to help their students to learn. In
the Soviet Union there is a much greater emphasis on the
theory of CBL, to the extent that the use of CBL was
postponed not only until the computer hardware was available
but also until suitable pedagogical theories were ready.
Although there is relatively less use of educational microcomputing in the Soviet Union than in the rest of Europe
(because of the lack of hardware), that which does exist is
well designed. It may lack the attractive gloss of
graphics, but the underlying professional approach shows
through. Given the Soviet interest in distance learning and

their experience of, and need for, technologies to extend the range of teaching, they are likely to make rapid advances in this area.

5.3 Training

Whatever the degree of integration of computer studies and CBL, whatever the learning style and emphasis on learning theory, there is little doubt that the key to successful educational computing is teacher training. Our experience over the last decade with CBL has shown that the long term assimilation of innovation needs strength in depth, and this means training. Relying on the continued presence of a scattered band of enthusiasts is an uncertain strategy, although it should be noted that one volunteer is worth ten pressed men or women! Much of the success of the French CBL experiment can be attributed to the centralised teacher training programme in which several hundreds of teachers were seconded for a year to attend a full time course in computing, informatics and CBL. By comparison the training in other countries has been minimal. There are few, if any, pre-service teacher training courses which include in their cores, a significant component on computer studies or the impact of microcomputers on curriculum and teaching methods.

If we are to achieve our aspirations for educational computing, which are, after all, supported by our various ministries and departments of education, then each country faces a massive training problem. We must simultaneously introduce the subject into the core of pre-service courses, and develop a programme of in-service workshops. This must be our highest priority. But if we are realistic, we must admit that whatever we do, it will come too late because microcomputers have already arrived in the classrooms in continental Europe.

Acknowledgements

As always, I must thank my friends and colleagues in the UK, Europe and North America for the continuing dialogues which generate the basis for such comparative studies. Without their help papers like this would be infinitely more difficult to write, and my subjective views much more suspect!

References

1. J.S.A.ANDERSON and J.FAY, Northern Ireland needs more micro awareness, Educational Computing, 1(7), 1980

2. L-E BJORK and B.SNAAR, Computers and curriculum development in Swedish secondary schools, in Tagg, E.D. (ed) Microcomputers in secondary education, North Holland, 1980

3. CET, Microcomputers in schools: survey report, Council for Education Technology and the Schools Council, London (mimeo), 1980

4. EDUCATIONAL COMPUTING Editorial, Survey reveals sorry state, 1(8), 1980

5. K.HAEFNER, Microcomputers and the future in German education, paper at the 2nd International Microcomputers in Education Congress, London.

6. R.HOOPER, National Development Programme in Computer Assisted Learning: final report of the Director, Council for Educational Technololgy, London, 1977

7. INRP, Language symbolique d'enseignement (LSE): Manual d'utilisation, Bulletin de liason l'informatique et l'Enseignement Secondaire Numero special (in French), 1975

8. T.JENSEN, Microcomputers in Danish secondary education, Paper at the 2nd International Microcomputers in Education Congress, London, 1980

9. W.MERCOUROFF, L'experience des 58 lycees, Education et Informatique, No.1, 1980

10. N.J.RUSHBY, E.B.JAMES, and J.S.A.ANDERSON, A three dimensional view of computer based learning in Continental Europe, Programmed Learning and Educational Technology 15(2), 1978

11. M.SACCO, Informatics in secondary education in France: teacher training, in Tagg, E.D. (ed) Microcomputers in Secondary Education, North Holland, 1978

13

COMPUTER LITERACY AND AWARENESS

D.C.Johnson

University of London

R.E.Anderson and T.P.Hansen,

Minnesota Educational Computing Consortium,

and D.L.Klassen

St. Olaf College

1. Introduction

The notion of Computer Literacy has received considerable attention in the past decade. The optional courses in the United Kingdom in the area of computer studies have a history dating back to the mid 60's and at present approximately 40% of the 6,000 secondary schools offer some formal coursework in this area. The British Computer Society Schools Committee has provided a focal point and leadership for curriculum recommendations (e.g. see [4]). The U.S. has a similar history as there have been a number of professional groups and individuals advocating school activities/curriculum orientated towards the development of pupils' understanding of computing and implications of this technology (e.g. see [5], [8], [9], [10], [11]).

Today, the 1980s, the widescale availability and impact of microprocessor technology in home, school, and the world of work suggests that schools which do not incorporate the opportunity for pupils to develop an understanding of, and the capability to deal with, this revolutionary technology are remiss in fulfilling their responsibility. While wide scale availability is at present a phenomenon characteristic of developed countries it is readily apparent that developing countries must also concern themselves with the educational implications as the ever decreasing costs of microcomputers suggest that even between the time of writing this paper and publication we will see small (only in size) machines available at a cost 50-80% less than today (from 500 pounds to less than 100 pounds).

What should the educated citizen know to be able to function as a contributing member of a society which utilizes computers in the home, business, industry, and government? Obviously, to attempt an answer to this question is very much like trying to answer the similar question of "what and how much mathematics?". In education we tend to suggest that while there may be some 'minimal level' of understanding it is also the goal that each child should be educated to his or her full potential. In the case of computing and the unknowns of what the future holds this means we have the obligation to develop an awareness of the technology including a knowledge of the special vocabulary, notions of both strengths and limitations, and an understanding of the issues which accompany computerization of tasks. To be computer literate implies comprehension and the ability to discuss computing concepts, applications, and issues intelligently. At a somewhat higher level, a functional level if you wish, the phrase includes the ability to actually use or identify new uses of computers in home and profession. Obviously, as indicated previously, it should be the goal of education to provide an opportunity for all pupils to reach a level of literacy commensurate with each individual's potential.

Where are we today? What is the state of knowledge of school pupils? What is being recommended? The next section of this paper describes some of the initial work in an attempt to assess pupils' knowledge and understanding in a broadly defined area of computer literacy. The research, supported by the National Science Foundation†, was conducted in Minnesota, U.S.A.

2. Computer literacy and awareness assessment

The Minnesota research project was designed to (1) collect baseline data regarding pupil knowledge and understandiong of computers, and (2) to determine the relative impact of the various computing or computer-related activities in schools on the development of computer knowledge and understanding. The research was conducted during the period 1977-1979 and the Final Report [7] reports on results from a teacher survey, over 3,500 teachers [1]; a field study, assessment and background information collected on over 1100 secondary pupils; and an experimental study, over 350 pupils.

Initial work of the project involved an extensive review of the available information regarding how different individuals and organisations viewed the phrase 'computer literacy' or 'computer awareness'. This enabled the research team to develop an empirical definition of the construct. This phase of the research resulted in a listing of 54 objectives in the cognitive domain under the categories of Hardware (H), 7 objectives; Programming and Algorithms (P), 8 objectives; Software and Data Processing (S), 13 objectives; Applications (A), 10 objectives; and Impact (I),

16 objectives; and 9 objectives in the affective domain in the areas of Attitude, Values, and Motivation (see [6] for a more complete discussion of the objectives). It is interesting to contrast this listing and the general topic headings and descriptions in the British Computer Society Schools Committee, 1979, recommendations.

The Minnesota research project designed a test, The Computer Literacy Questionnaire [7] to assess a subset of the objectives. For purposes of this paper we will restrict the discussion to the cognitive objectives and in particular those which were included in the Questionnaire (34 out of 54 objectives were assessed). The objectives and corresponding test items are reported in Tables 1-5.

Table 1

COMPUTER LITERACY
HARDWARE (H): OBJECTIVES AND TEST ITEMS(N=8)

Objectives (note (a))	Item Number(s)
*H.1.1 Identify the five major components of a computer: input equipment, memory unit, control unit, arithmetic unit, output equipment.	33
*H.1.2 Identify the basic operation of a computer system. Input of data or information - Processing of data or information - Output of data or information.	34
*H.1.3 Distinguish between hardware and software.	32,35
*H.1.4 Identify how a person can access a computer; e.g. 1. via a keyboard terminal a. at site of computer b. at any distance via telephone lires 2. via punched or marked cards 3. via other magnetic media (tape, diskette)	16,19
*H.1.5 Recognize the rapid growth of computer hardware since the 1940's.	31
*H.2.1 Determine that the basic components function as an interconnected system under the control of a stored program	36

developed **by a person.**

*H.2.2 <u>Compare</u> computer processing and storage   not
       capabilities to the human brain listing   assessed
       some general similarities and
       differences.

Items (<u>note</u> (<u>b</u>))

16. In order to use a computer you would have to be in the same building as the computer. (T, F, I don't know).

19. In order to use any computer you would have to use a telephone. (T, F, I don't know).

31. The decade of first extensive manufacturing of computers was: a) 1860's b) 1890's c) 1920's d) 1950's e) I don't know

32. Computer software is a term describing: a) computer programs b) electronic components encased in soft plastic or rubber c) people who work with computers d) mechanical and electronic parts of a computer system e) I don't know

33. In addition to input and output equipment, computers contain: a) terminals, paper, transistors b) memory units, control units, arithmetic units c) printers and typewriters d) telephones, keyboards, television screens e) I don't know

34. A computer <u>system</u> is best described as: a) processing b) programming, input, and output c) input and output d) input, processing, and output e) I don't know

35. The physical parts of a computer are referred to as: a) programs b) hardware c) software d) manuals e) I don't know

36. When in operation, a computer: a) follows a set of instructions written by people b) thinks just like a person c) recalls answers from memory d) translates data from digital to analog code e) I don't know

a. The objectives with an * are designated as core and were assessed in Part II of the Computer Literacy Questionnaire.

b. To save space, the format here is slightly different from the actual test.

Table 2

COMPUTER LITERACY
PROGRAMMING AND ALGORITHMS(P):
OBJECTIVES AND TEST ITEMS(N=5)

NOTE: The student should be able to accomplish objectives
1.2 - 2.5 when the algorithm is expressed as a set
of English language instructions and in the form
of a computer program.

Objectives (note (a))	Item Number
P.1.1 Recognize the definition of "algorithm".	
*P.1.2 Follow and give the correct output for a simple algorithm.	45 (English item) 47 (Programming item)
*P.1.3 Given a simple algorithm explain what it accomplishes (i.e. interpret and generalize).	48 (Programming item)
*P.2.1 Modify a simple algorithm to accomplish a new but related task.	46(Flow Chart) 49(Programming item)
P.2.2 Detect logic errors in an algorithm.	
P.2.3 Correct errors in an improperly functioning algorithm.	
P.2.4 Develop an algorithm for solving a specific problem.	
P.2.5 Develop an algorithm which can be used to solve a set of similar problems.	

Items (note (b))

45. Choose the correct result for the procedure described
below:

    1. List the three names Brown, Anderson and Crane
       in alphabetical order.
    2. Remove the last name from the list
    3. If only one name is left, stop. Otherwise
       go on to step 4.

4. List the remaining names in reverse order.
5. Go back to step 2

Output: a)Anderson,Brown,Crane; b) Brown; c) Anderson,
Brown; d) Anderson; e) I don't know

46. A flowchart to determine the weekly wages of employees
in a bakery is shown below. Employees are paid $4 per
hour up to 40 hours per week.

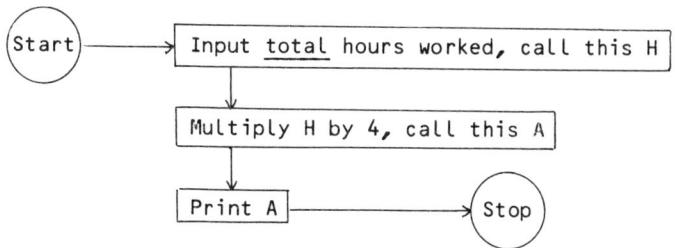

Employees are now to be paid "time-and-a-half"($6 per
hour) for overtime (hours worked over 40). How would you
complete the flowchart below to include overtime pay?
Select answer a, b, c, d, or e.

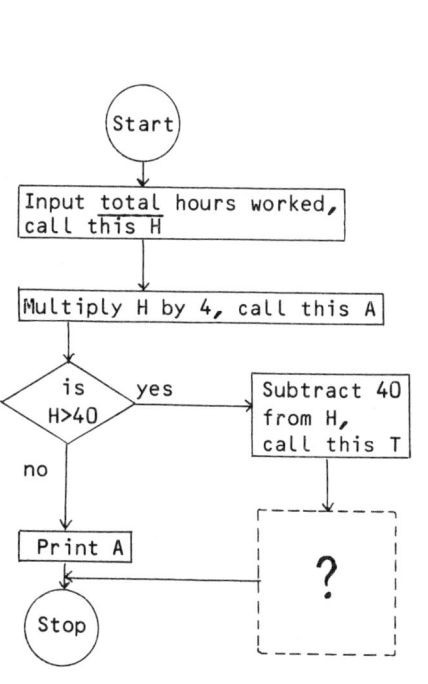

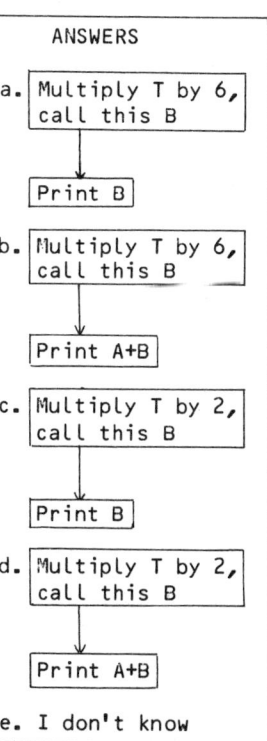

47. Choose the correct output for the computer program shown below:

```
1  LET A = 3
2  LET B = 4
3  LET C = A
4  LET B = C
5  LET A = B
6  PRINT A,B
7  END
```

Output: a) 3 4; b) 4 3; c) 3 3; d) 4 4;
e) I don't know

48. When run on a computer, the following program will:

```
1   INPUT A, B, C, D, E
2   LET S = A+B+C+D+E
3   LET M = S/5
4   PRINT S,M
5   END
```

a) Calculate the sum of five input values
b) Calculate the average of five input values
c) Print the sum and average of five input values
d) all of the above
e) I don't know

49. This program instructs the computer to count by two:

```
10 LET M = 0
20 LET M = M + 2
30 PRINT M
40 IF M < 100 THEN 20
50 END
```

Which change will produce a program which can be used to count by A? (For example, A=3, 5, or 8).

a) 5 READ A   b) 5 LET M = A   c) 5 INPUT A
   7 DATA 3,5,8   30 PRINT A   20 LET M = M+A

d) 5 LET X = A   e) I don't know
   20 LET M = X+A

a. The objectives with an * are designated as core and were assessed in Part II of the Computer Literacy Questionnaire.

b. To save space, the format here is slightly different from the actual test.

Table 3

COMPUTER LITERACY
SOFTWARE AND DATA PROCESSING(S):
OBJECTIVES AND TEST ITEMS(N=8)

	Objectives (note (a))	Item Number(s)
S.1.1	Identify the fact that we communicate with computers through a binary code.	
S.1.2	Identify the need for data to be organized if it is to be useful.	
S.1.3	Identify the fact that information is data which has been given meaning.	
S.1.4	Identify the fact that data is a coded mechanism for communication.	
S.1.5	Identify the fact that communication is the transmission of information via coded messages.	
*S.1.6	Identify the fact that data processing involves the transformation of data by means of a set of predefined rules.	40
*S.1.7	Recognize that a computer needs instructions to operate.	37
*S.1.8	Recognize that a computer gets instructions from a program written in a programming language.	38,41
*S.1.9	Recognize that a computer is capable of storing a program and data.	39,43
*S.1.10	Recognize that computers process data by searching, sorting, deleting, updating, summarizing, moving, etc.	42
*S.2.1	Select an appropriate attribute for ordering of data for a particular task.	44
S.2.2	Design an elementary data structure for a given application (that is, provide order for the data).	
S.2,3	Design an elementary coding system for a given application.	

21

37. Computers cannot run without: a) blinking lights
b) keyboards c) instructions d) all of the above
e) I don't know

38. In order to program a computer, a person: a) can use any
English language words b) can use any English or foreign
language words c) must use programming language numbers,
not words d) must use the words from a programming
language e) I don't know

39. At any given moment, a computer's memory unit can store:
a) programs b) data c) answers d) all of the above
e) I don't know

40. Data processing is best described as: a) the collection
of data b) producing reports c) manipulating data
according to instructions d) using punched cards in a
keypunch machine e) I don't know

41. A computer program is a: a) course on computers b) set
of instructions to control the computer c) computer
generated presentation d) piece of computer hardware
e) I don't know

42. Computer processing of data may involve: a) searching
b) summarizing c) deleting d) all of the above e) I
don't know

43. The computer must have two types of information to
solve a problem: a) the problem and the answer b) the
name of the program and user number c) the data and
the instructions d) all of the above e) I don't know

44. A newspaper publisher has the following information
about subscribers stored in the computer. They are
name, address and renewal date. How would you arrange
the information to be most useful to the delivery
person? a) ordered listing by address b) ordered listing
by renewal dates c) alphabetical listing of streets
d) ordered listing by zip code e) I don't know

a. The objectives with an * are designated as core and were
assessed in Part II of the Computer Literacy
Questionnaire.

b. To save space, the format here is slightly different
from the actual test.

Table 4

COMPUTER LITERACY
APPLICATIONS (A): OBJECTIVES AND TEST ITEMS (N=15)

Objectives (note (a))	Item Number(s)

*A.1.1 Recognize specific uses of   1,2,3,4,5
computers in some of the
following:
a. medicine
b. law enforcement
c. education
d. engineering
e. business
f. transportation
g. military defense systems
h. weather prediction
i. recreation
j. government
k. the library
l. creative arts

*A.1.2 Identify the fact that there are
many programming languages
suitable for a particular
application for business or
science.

*A.1.3 Recognize that the following activities   26,27
are among the major types of applications
of the computer:
a. information storage and retrieval
b. simulation and modelling
c. process control - decision-making
d. computation
e. data processing

*A.1.4 Recognize that computers are generally   6,21
good at information processing tasks
that benefit from:
a. speed
b. accuracy
c. repetitiveness

*A.1.5 Recognize that some limiting considerations   29
for using computers are:
a. cost
b. software availability
c. storage capacity

*A.1.6 Recognize the basic features of a   20,30
computerized information system.

*A.2.1 <u>Determine</u> how computers can assist   9
        the consumer.

*A.2.2 <u>Determine</u> how computers can assist in   7,8
        a decision-making process.

A.2.3   <u>Assess</u> the feasibility of potential
        applications.

A.2.4   <u>Develop</u> a new application.

<u>Items</u> (<u>note</u> (<u>b</u>))

1. Police sometimes use computers to help identify stolen
   cars. (T, F, I don't know)

2. Most hospitals give injections by computer. (T, F,
   I don't know)

3. Computers <u>cannot</u> be used to assist in teaching English
   grammar. (T, F, I don't know)

4. Computers are not really used very much yet except by
   scientists. (T, F, I don't know)

5. Government officials use computers to store and retrieve
   large amounts of information about citizens. (T, F,
   I don't know)

6. People often use computers to store large amounts of
   information they wish to use over and over again.
   (T, F, I don't know)

7. Computers help people make decisions by providing
   correct answers to any question. (T, F, I don't know)

8. Computers help people make decisions by telling them
   if their problem is important. (T, F, I don't know)

9. Computers have been used to make more information and
   products available to the consumer. (T, F, I don't know)

20. In order to use a computer a person must know how to
    program. (T, F, I don't know)

21. Computers are not good for tasks that require: a) speed
    b) accuracy c) intuition d) something to be done over
    and over again e) I don't know.

26. A basic use of computers in libraries involves:
    a) information storage and retrieval b) simulation and
    modelling c) process control d) computation e) I don't
    know.

27. A basic use for computers in the design of airplanes is:
    a) simulation and modelling b) process control c) making
    reservations d) keeping inventory e) I don't know.

29. Which of the following is a limiting consideration for
    using computers? a) cost b) software availability
    c) storage capacity d) all of the above e) I don't know.

30. Which is not a characteristic of most information
    systems?
    a) a large volume of information is stored and used
    b) the information is organized c) the basic purpose
    is to provide reports and summaries of the data
    d) they contain only aphabetic data e) I don't know.

a. The objectives with an * are designated as core and were
   assessed in Part II of the Computer Literacy
   Questionnaire.
b. To save space, the format here is slightly different from
   the actual test.

Table 5

COMPUTER LITERACY
IMPACT (I): OBJECTIVES AND TEST ITEMS (N=13)

Objectives (note (a))	Item Number(s)
*I.1.1 Distinguish among the following careers: a. keypuncher/keyoperator b. computer operator c. computer programmer d. systems analyst e. computer scientist	23,24,25
*I.1.2 Recognize that computers are used to commit a wide variety of serious crimes but especially stealing money and stealing information.	10

*I.1.3 <u>Recognize</u> that identification codes   11
<u>(numbers)</u> and passwords are a primary
means for restricting use of computer
systems, of computer programs, and of
data files.

I.1.4 <u>Recognize</u> that procedures for detecting
computer-based crimes are not well
developed.

*I.1.5 <u>Identify</u> some advantages or disadvantages   28
of a data base containing personal
information on a large number of people
(e.g. the list might include value for
research and potential for privacy
invasion).

I.1.6 <u>Recognize</u> several regulatory procedures:
e.g. privilege to review one's own file
and restrictions on use of universal
personal identifiers, which help to
insure the integrity of personal data
files.

*I.1.7 <u>Recognize</u> that most "privacy problems"   13
are characteristic of large information
files whether or not they are
computerized.

*I.1.8 <u>Recognize</u> that computerization both   14
increases and decreases employment.

*I.1.9 <u>Recognize</u> that computerization both   12
personalizes and impersonalizes
procedures in fields such as
education.

*I.1.10 <u>Recognize</u> that computerization can lead   18
to both greater independence and
dependence upon one's tools.

*I.1.11 <u>Recognize</u> that while computers do not   17
have the mental capacity that humans
do, through techniques such as
artificial intelligence, computers
have been able to modify their own
instruction set and do many of the
information processing tasks that
humans do.

*I.1.12 <u>Recognize</u> that alleged "computer   22
mistakes" are usually mistakes made
by people.

*I.2.1   <u>Plan</u> a strategy for tracing and   not
        correcting a computer related error   assessed
        such as a billing error.

I.2.2   <u>Explain</u> how computers make public
        surveillance more feasible.

*I.2.3   <u>Recognize</u> that even though a person   15
        does not go near a computer, he or she
        is affected indirectly because the
        society is different in many sectors
        as a consequence of computerizastion.

I.2.4   <u>Explain</u> how computers can be used to
        impact the distribution and use of
        economic and political power.

<u>Items</u> (<u>note</u> (<u>b</u>))

10. Computers are used to commit crimes, especially stealing
money and stealing or falsifying information. (T, F,
I don't know)

11. Identification numbers and passwords are a primary means
for restricting undesired access to computer files. (T,
F, I don't know)

12. Use of computers in education always results in less
personal treatment of students. (T, F, I don't know)

13. Privacy is an issue with files containing personal
information about people. (T, F, I don't know)

14. The increased use of computers in our society both
eliminates and creates jobs. (T, F, I don't know)

15. Almost all people in our society are affected in
some way by computers. (T, F, I don't know)

17. Computers are able to think in every way just like
people. (T, F, I don't know)

18. Using computers can free one to do more creative
tasks, but this may lead to more dependence upon
machines. (T, F, I don't know)

22. If your charge account bill has an error, it was
probably caused by:
a) breakdown of the computer b) mistakes made by
people c) poor design of the computer c) general
weaknesses of machines e) I don't know

23. The main duty of a computer programmer is to:
a) operate a computer b) prepare instructions for
a computer c) schedule jobs for a computer
d) design computers e) I don't know

24. The computer related job closest to that of a
typist is: a) computer operator b) keypunch operator
c) systems analyst d) computer programmer e) I don't
know

25. Which of the following persons is the most likely to
be associated with the design of computers? a) keypunch
operator b) computer operator c) computer programmer
d) computer scientist e) I don't know

28. The most questionable use of large computer files is:
a) government planning b) research c) checking on
people d) administration of social programs e) I don't
know

a. The objectives with an * are designated as core and were
assessed in Part II of the Computer Literacy
Questionnaire.

b. To save space, the format here is slightly different from
the actual test.

```
                          SCORING KEY

                  COGNITIVE PORTION (PART 2)
               OF COMPUTER LITERACY QUESTIONNAIRE

   1. a      8. b     15. a     22. b     29. d     36. a     43. c
   2. b      9. a     16. b     23. b     30. d     37. c     44. a
   3. b     10. a     17. b     24. b     31. d     38. d     45. b
   4. b     11. a     18. a     25. d     32. a     39. d     46. d
   5. a     12. b     19. b     26. a     33. b     40. c     47. c
   6. a     13. a     20. b     27. a     34. d     41. b     48. d
   7. b     14. a     21. c     28. c     35. b     42. d     49. e
```

The composite cognitive portion of the test (49 items) has a
reliability of .90 and the distribution of item difficulties
and item discriminations were both broad and fairly uniform
[3].

The Questionnaire was used in a field study for which
complete data were available from 1106 pupils (in 51

classrooms). Of these, 929 pupils were in classrooms which had some type of planned computing activity (e.g.,CAL, programming, computer appreciation, etc.). Figure 1 shows the relative performance on the various subsections of the test.

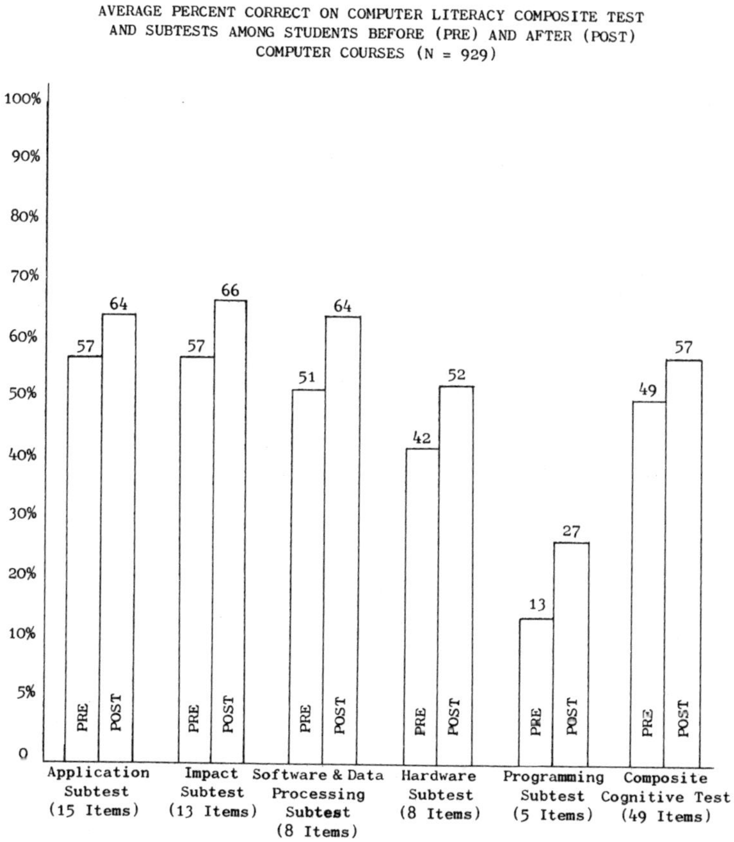

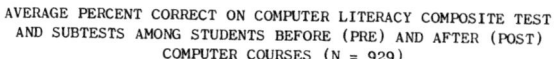

AVERAGE PERCENT CORRECT ON COMPUTER LITERACY COMPOSITE TEST
AND SUBTESTS AMONG STUDENTS BEFORE (PRE) AND AFTER (POST)
COMPUTER COURSES (N = 929)

Figure 1. Average percent correct on computer literacy composite test and subtests among students before (pre) and after (post) computer courses (N=929)

These data suggest that if one accepts the objectives and corresponding items as appropriate (note again that the test has been revised), then even with these pupils who have had some exposure to computing activities there is room for improvement as average performance on the final composite cognitive computer literacy test was only 27.9 or 57 percent correct.

3. Epilogue

What does all this mean? Where and how should computer literacy/awarenss be developed? The Minnesota research tells us that while exposure to computing in different aspects of schooling does give pupils some insights, there is still much that could be done. In particular, there is a need for more planned activity which emphasises the specific computing objectives. These can take place in a number of disciplines (and some objectives are more appropriate for specific subject areas, e.g. programming and algorithms are a natural part of mathematics and aspects of impact and issues certainly fit into an up-to-date social studies curriculum). However, the overall program needs to be coordinated and attempts made to ensure a range of activities which will result in an education of a comprehensive and cohesive nature.

References

1. R.ANDERSON, T.HANSEN, D.JOHNSON and D.KLASSEN, Acceptance and rejection of instructional computing by secondary school teachers, Sociology of Work and Occupations, May 1979.

2. R.ANDERSON, T.HANSEN, D.JOHNSON and D.KLASSEN, The Minnesota Computer Literacy and Awareness Assessment (test), Minnesota Educational Computing Consortium, St. Paul, Minnesota (U.S.), 1979.

3. R.ANDERSON, D.KLASSEN, D.JOHNSON and T.HANSEN, The Minnesota Literacy Tests: A Technical Report on the MECC Computer Literacy Field Study, Minnesota Educational Computing Consortium, St.Paul, Minnesota (U.S.), 1979.

4. BRITISH COMPUTER SOCIETY SCHOOLS COMMITTEE, Syllabuses for the Future, British Computer Society, London 1979.

5. CBMS (Conference Board for the Mathematical Sciences), Recommendations Regarding Computers in High School Education, Washington, D.C., 1972.

6. D.JOHNSON, R.ANDERSON, T.HANSEN and D.KLASSEN, Computer Literacy - what is it? , Mathematics Teacher, Vol.73 (Feb. 1980), pp.91-96.

7. D.KLASSEN, R.ANDERSON, T.HANSEN and D.JOHNSON, A Study of Computer Use and Literacy in Science Education, (supported by Grant No. SED 77-18658), Minnesota Educational Computing Consortium, St.Paul, Minnesota, 1980.
(Note: the questionnaire referred to in this publication has been revised, the most recent version is [2] above. It has been used in the Minnesota Statewide assessment program, approximately 6000 pupils, and data are now being analysed.)

8. D.MICHAEL, The Unprepared Society, New York, Basic Books,Inc., 1968.

9. A.MOLNAR, The next great Crisis in American education: computer literacy, The Journal, July/August, 1978, pp.35-39.

10. D.MOURSUND, What is Computer Literacy?, Oregon Computing Teacher, Oregon Council for Computer Education, Vol.2, No. 2, June 1975, p.17.

11. NCSM (National Council of Supervisors of Mathematics), Position statements on basic skills, Mathematics Teacher, vol.71, (Feb 1978), pp.147-52.

This paper was presented at the International Congress for Mathematical Education, ICME, Berkely, California, U.S.A., August 1980, and again at the British Education Research Association, BERA, Annual Conference, Cardiff, Wales, September, 1980.

♦This paper was prepared with the support of National Science Foundation Grant No. SED 77-18658. Any opinions, findings, conclusions or recommendations expressed are those of the authors and do not necessarily reflect the views of the National Science Foundation.

HERTFORDSHIRE COMPUTER MANAGED MATHEMATICS PROJECT (HCMMP)

W.Tagg

Advisory Unit for Computer Based Education
Hertfordshire County Council

1. Introduction

This project is just one of the concerns of the Advisory Unit for Computer Based Education in Hatfield but it is different from the others in two major respects. First, because of the level of external funding that it has been able to attract, it is bigger than any other Advisory Unit project, and secondly its clasroom impact has been much greater. This paper, as well as describing the details of the project, examines some of the reasons why it is sometimes regarded as a threat to teachers rather than an aid.

2. History

The origins of HCMMP go back to 1972 when Hatfield School, under its own initiative, decided to invest in a computer managed scheme for early secondary mathematics by using funds that had been set aside for a language laboratory in their new building. At that time, the 11+ examination was only newly abolished and the mathematics syllabus had not settled down from the upheaval created by the vogue for "the New Maths". The end of the 11+ had meant that primary schools were no longer working towards an implied common syllabus so that children were arriving at secondary school with a variety of mathematical backgrounds. In addition, secondary heads were reluctant to stream according to ability when children first reached 11. They had no accurate method of achieving this and the climate of opinion was against it.

Many mathematics teachers were sympathetic to the concepts of mixed ability teaching, but felt that the hierarchical nature of mathematics education posed special problems. In 1974, T.J. Fletcher [1] put it this way:

> "Developments such as the teaching of mixed ability groups, the integration of the teaching of mathematics with other subject areas, and the adoption of various methods of self-paced

learning, all raise problems. We may accept the
validity of the educational objectives, but there
are many difficulties to overcome if mathematics
is to be taught within such a framework without
any impairment of the pupils' performance by
previously accepted criteria."

It was because Richard Hooper saw the need for new solutions
to new problems that HCMMP received a major NDPCAL grant in
1973 and it was its continuing success beyond the period of
external funding that persuaded the Department of Industry
to award a grant under the MAP programme to enable the
software to be rewritten for a microcomputer.

3. What is HCMMP?

Computer Managed Learning is still not a very well defined
term so it is necessary to spell out in a little detail just
what HCMMP involves. Those who require more information
should write to the Advisory Unit for further details.

HCMMP originally consisted of two schemes: ESYMRK was a two
year structured course based on worksheets but with a
computer to do some of the marking, scheduling and record
keeping; and SAM was a computerised scheme for providing
worksheets to give practice in arithmetical skills. SAM has
suffered by being misunderstood and by being the subject of
philosophical quarrels and has died (or at least gone into
long term hibernation). However ESYMRK is still alive and
well and most of what is written here is about ESYMRK.

The two year course is divided into modules each of which
lasts from two to three weeks. In one class, the children
are normally working on the same module, although clearly
this will not be the case during the changeover from one
module to the next. Within a module, children work at their
own pace, but the fact that all are working on the same
topic enables the advantages of a to leap from topic to
topic as he or she helps one group and then another. At the
end of the module, some children will have progressed
further than others, but the work is organised so that
beyond a defined cut-off point the work is of an enrichment
nature so that the slower pupil, who has not had time to go
to the end of the module of work, is not at a disadvantage
when the current work is used at a later stage. At least
that is the theory, but in practice of course much depends
on the skill and energy of the teacher just as with any
other scheme.

3.1 Role of the computer

The trouble with any individualised teaching scheme is that other things being equal, the marking load is significantly increased. This is because it is much easier to mark in circumstances where it is possible to memorise the questions, correct answers and usual pitfalls based on the first few that are marked. Since the marking burden in mathematics is greater than in many other subjects, teachers often resort to self marking techniques and students all suffer. Proponents of self marking argue that the immediacy which it brings compensates for its disadvantages and it is certainly true that a short turn-round time has been one of the on-going objectives of the project.

Work is structured so that a worksheet is either completely marked by computer or is completely marked by the teacher. Teacher marked worksheets contain the more open ended types of questions and the computer marked sheets, although not multiple choice questions in the traditional sense, are of the type where anticipated wrong responses are relatively easy to find. As well as the correct answers to these worksheets, the computer stores any anticipated wrong answers together with comments for the student. In this way the student gets his work marked as if by a very conscientious teacher, and the teacher gets a mark list.

Sometimes of course the student's problem requires teacher intervention and if the computer's comment is 'see your teacher', the teacher's mark list contains a symbol to indicate that this message has been given.

4. Reactions to the project

Although the project has been in existence now for nearly nine years and although teachers have been actively involved in the development of the teaching strategy, course and worksheets, there is still some opposition to the project - some of which is from successful teachers. It is interesting to speculate on the reasons for this, although what is required is a full scale independent investigation.

There can be no doubt that some teaching styles suit some teachers better than others and that HCMMP, like many individualised schemes, demands a reasonably well organised teacher. The syllabus and worksheet content is sometimes criticised, and why not, but it is difficult to see how more teacher involvement could have been used in its creation. Any textbook or teaching project has its critics, yet despite the undoubted success of the project there have been times when criticism has been quite unexpected. Maybe this is because CML represents a complete take-over on the part of the computer, with the teacher playing a significantly different (although just as important) role, whereas CAL is usually much more of an add-on exercise.

5. Technical matters

Initially a mainframe computer using a suite of programs in COBOL was used for the processing and this meant a time critical courier service to get the work back to the children for their next lesson. In 1979, the computing side was redeveloped for a disk based 380Z microcomputer. This time, programming was in FORTRAN with the object code of the largest program running in 48K. Although much of the work still operates centrally using an 8 inch disk based system at the Advisory Unit, half a dozen schools now operate independently with five and a quarter inch disk based systems operating in their own schools. This has provided the opportunity for the development of a immediate response.

Since the start of the project, data capture has been via marksensing using a Data Recognition document reader for the mainframe and marksensed card readers for the microcomputer version. Despite their limitations, marksensed cards have provided the means of giving a quick cheap turn-round. Since the children are using them every day, they quickly learn to cope and although errors are never completely eliminated, what matters is that the teacher has a method of coping with the bulk of the class. Any odd child who falls through the system is dealt with manually, in fact the system has always remained sufficiently flexible for the teacher to intervene and countermand the computer's instructions.

6. Future developments

The rate of development for Computer Managed Learning Schemes is likely to be limited more by their rate of acceptance than by technical advances. Software, of course, remains expensive, but the continuing drop in hardware costs means that we now have available economic solutions to class teaching where hitherto the marking of the work has been the problem. There remains a question mark over the long term future of marksensed input, not because it does not work, but because outside education it does not seem to have found a place.

References

1. T.J.FLETCHER, Trends in Education, October 1974

DESIGN AND EVALUATION
OF EDUCATIONAL SOFTWARE
FOR GROUP PRESENTATION

Rosemary Fraser

College of St. Mark and St. John
Plymouth, England

1. Introduction

This paper is concerned with the design and evaluation of
computer programs that will offer the teacher a resource
that he will welcome as a useful aid to be used with a whole
class, or with a group of pupils. Computer programs exhibit
signs of intelligence by the fact that they can respond to
signals from both teacher and pupils. Although the responses
appear very restricted compared to the range of responses
possible between teacher and student or between student and
student, nevertheless the communication that is possible
offers many new approaches to learning. Thus classroom
activities, discussion, lessons, investigation etc. can be
built from the interaction between teacher, pupils and
computer program, shown in figure 1. Some of the
difficulties experienced when writing material for this
situation are outlined in this paper.

2. Computer-teacher communication

Perhaps the most vital problem is establishing easy
communication between the computer program and the teacher.
The computer has talents that can be employed to produce
displays of data in many different visual presentations, it
can also be used to set up problems for investigation; it
can create environments and produce pseudo-random effects.
Combinations of these and other possibilites offer very rich
opportunities for learning. The teacher needs to consider
these possibilities in relationship to the content and
management of all his material. Being able to respond
quickly to attitudes, reactions and situations because of
his intelligence and experience, he remains the creator of
the total environment. Pupils interact in the environment
in a very complex manner which no machine can recognise and
react to as sensitively as the teacher can. The situation
has been illustrated in figure 2 as two objects, one
constant and one changing, linked by a communication channel
which depends on both objects. The constant part of the
situation is the finished computer program from which the
teacher can select material and the changing part is the use

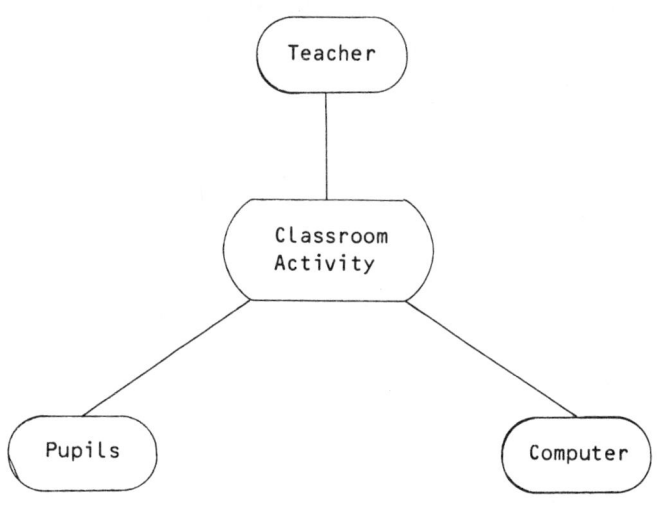

Figure 1.

of that program, which depends both on the selection made
and the individual teacher's personality and approach to
teaching.

The DRIVING SYSTEM is characterised by the control and
flexibility offered to the driver from the computer program.
The communications channel functions efficiently if the
driver not only understands and can operate the driving
controls but also on the performance of the driving system
itself. The use of a program as part of a lesson requires
that the communication has an easy flow and does not place
unnecessary demands on the teacher who wishes to react to
many other stimuli. It is no mean task to devise a system
that allows a teacher or any user of the program easy access
to all its options while ensuring that at any moment the
choice of alternatives is sufficiently restricted to
minimise confusion and delay in presentation which tends to
happen when the choice is too open. In other words, there
is an inherent tension between range and flexibility of a
program on the one hand and its simplicity and clarity on
the other. The designer needs to arrange or collect together
options that will have common characteristics linked to the
educational objectives of the teacher's use of the program;
simple memory aids can be introduced at the design stage so
that the teacher is always able to recognise quickly where
he has reached. The teacher needs to know to which signals

the program will respond without a long painful dialogue conducted in a 'Twenty Questions' quiz form.

There is no known best way to define a choice structure, and much research is required. However we see great advantages in the user having a clear overview of all the choices as well as assistance by subdivision of these choices in a way very sympathetic to the teaching. One way of providing this overview is to represent the control information in graphical form. DRIVECHARTS [1] are one method that we have devised. They are used with several of the ITMA [2] programs and have proved successful in the classroom. The charts are made up of three symbolic elements named DECISION POINTS, ROUTES and FEATURES; they represent a 'gastronomic tour' of the possibilities in that ROUTES are selected and FEATURES (a type of menu) chosen as they occur.

3. Exploiting the computer's talents

Great stress has been made so far on the communication channel for the program's use; now we shall turn briefly to the (constant object) in figure 2 from which we see that another major problem for the designer of educational software is to decide how to exploit the computer's talents to produce an educational aid.

Initial attempts to discuss this aspect appear in articles in the ITMA newsletters [2] and further detailed work is being undertaken. One task is to identify the computer's talents. A second, more difficult task, is to find successful combinations to offer the teacher. A combination must be flexible enough to be useful to teachers with many different styles and approaches. In creating a teaching unit the designer will see a whole range of possible extensions so there is a danger that dominance by computer power will distort the educational objectives of the material. One way of giving wide opportunities and minimising confusion is illustrated in the DRIVECHARTS where one FEATURE selection allows the teacher to choose from a clearly defined set of possibilities. This idea can be extended by the designer offering the teachers interchangeable sets of FEATURES, or setting up variations on this theme by building in offered alternatives. This has considerable advantages because the software is protected, flexibility is increased, and the control of the program is consistent. This is really very similar to the teacher's normal task of bringing together a selection of material to form the activities he considers most suitable. It is difficult to present this idea clearly without digressing into detailed descriptions. Each FEATURE allows certain conditions to be set — an alternative FEATURE offered to the teacher would have to 'fit' into the system, thus its behaviour would be defined by this system position

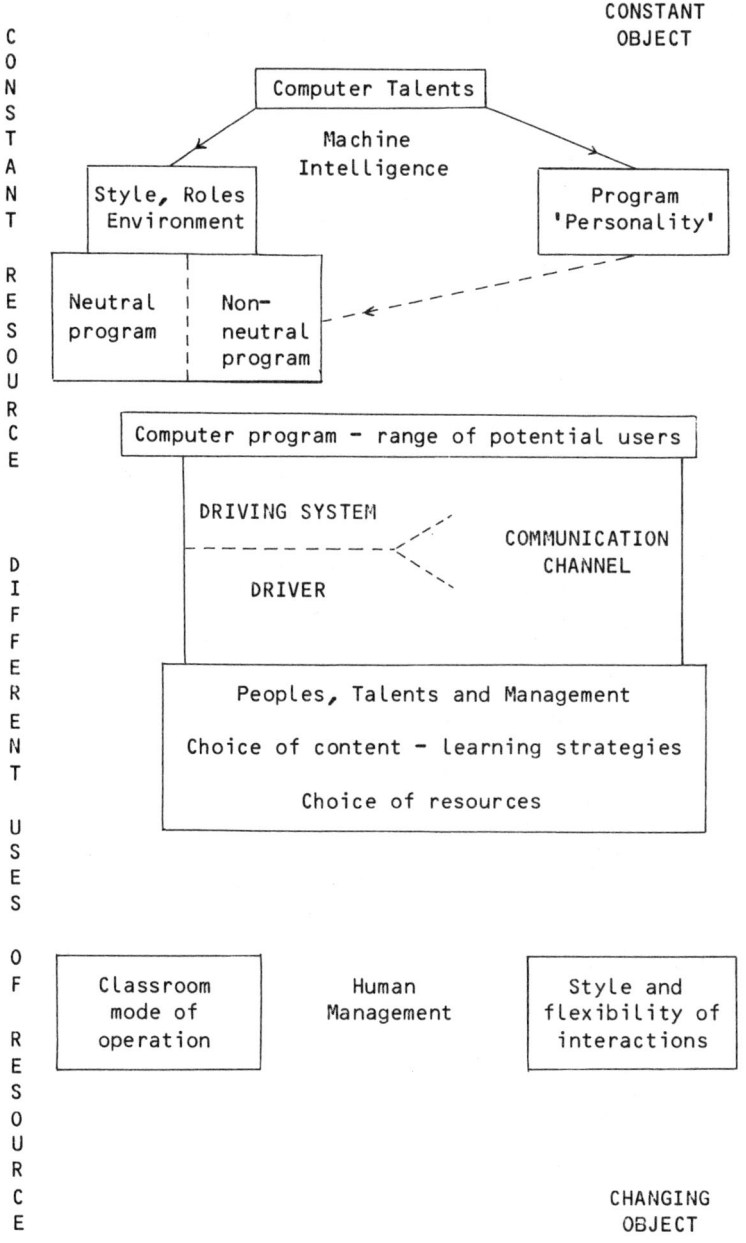

Figure 2.

but it could allow alternative conditions to be set.

Once sufficient experience in the production of educational software for classroom use has been built up, it will be possible to make good use of very sophisticated design tools that are already emerging, for example the SMALLTALK system from Xerox PALO ALTO Research Laboratories, California, U.S.A. It is inevitable that advanced design tools will be created by computer scientists − it is however the teacher and educator who will need to create the curriculum material. There is a very real danger that sophisticated design tools will not be easily accessible to the educators unless good liaison between them and the computer scientist is established.

4. Evaluation

Evaluation of computer programs used in the classroom brings us to figure 2 again. Looking at the 'changeable object' we realise this is the familiar problem of evaluating development of any new curriculum material. In the case of the computer material there is the added problem of acclimatising the teacher to the technology. We have developed a system of integrated evaluation alongside the development of material. Information is collected by:
    (1) Teacher's comments and observations. (Before and after).
    (2) Pupil's work produced.
    (3) Pupil interviews.
    (4) Observation of complete lessons
        by experienced observers. e.g. Video tapes and SCAN.
The class observations are done over a period of time, with lessons with and without the computer. This also enables pupils to become less self conscious. In this connection, SCAN [4], a Systematic Classroom Analysis Notation − developed in conjunction with Nottingham University, has proved extremely valuable in increasing teachers' and observers' awareness of the classroom interaction patterns and different teaching styles. The report [4] gives detailed comments on observed teachers styles, and the changes observed when computer programs have been used as part of the lesson.

These trials are only initial explorations and certainly no conclusions can be reached. They do however make very interesting reading and point to the fact that the computer may well offer a chance to assist and extend a teacher's ability to communicate with his pupils and motivate them to respond and express their thoughts.

5. Conclusion

One clear message is emerging from our experience to date.
Current technology is barely adequate for what we wish to
explore but we can learn a great deal about classroom use of
this technology by writing programs within its capabilities.
What we learn will certainly be helpful in creating material
for the sophisticated machines of the future. The true lack
of experience is in using computers in the classroom so we
need programs to help us gain this now. This creates a
dilemma as researchers also need to be exploring and
developing the potential of tomorrow's school machines which
are already in the research laboratory. However with
adequate resources it should be possible to move forward on
both fronts simultaneously and the most productive outcome
will be obtained if a programme of teacher training can be
developed that links together the classroom and the research
laboratory. A teacher training model (that looks towards
this possibility) has been described elsewhere [5]. It
suggests a material development loop and also a teacher
development loop that complement each other in growth.

It is a fascinating exercise to try to employ the computer
as a partner in the classroom. For any partnership to work a
great deal of understanding is needed: the systematic study
of what happens in the classroom is an essential part of
obtaining this understanding.

References

1. R.FRASER, H.BURKHARDT and C.WELLS, How DRIVECHARTS Work,
   College of St. Mark and St. John, Plymouth.

2. ITMA PROJECT NEWSLETTERS, (Ed. C. Wells). College of St.
   Mark and St. John, Plymouth.

3. A.KAY and A.GOLDBERG, Smalltalk Systems, Xerox PALO ALTO
   Research Laboratories,California,U.S.A.

4. T.BEEBY, H.BURKHARDT and R.FRASER, SCAN — a Systematic
   Classroom Analysis Notation for Mathematics Lessons,
   Shell Centre for Mathematical Education, Nottingham.

5. R.FRASER, Microcomputers and Teacher Education,
   Proceedings of the International Congress on Mathematical
   Education, Berkeley, California, 1980.

PEDAGOGICAL ISSUES
IN DESIGNING PROGRAMS

R.Lewis

Chelsea College, London

1. Introduction

Knowing the kind of confusion which can arise in readers'
minds when the acronym CAL (computer-assisted learning) is
used, it may be useful to propose a simplistic view of the
various uses of computers in education. In North America the
word 'instruction' is used to mean 'teaching' and /or
'learning' and this lack of discrimination is the root cause
of rather serious misunderstandings. It is important to
distinguish clearly between the computer in teacher mode and
the computer in resource mode. What is expected of the
programs, how the student perceives his interaction, the
relationship of the computer to other teaching or learning
forms - all are fundamentally affected.

It is possible to draw a distinction between the roles by
asking a simple question "Is the computer (program)
assessing the student?" to which one can answer 'yes' or
'no' at least in terms of the computer's predominant role.
The answer 'yes' (implying a need for the kind of system
shown in figure 1) gives rise to concern since the available
models of learner and subject matter content are very crude,
even non-existent, at present. Yet the essence of good
teaching includes some appreciation of what the learner does
and doesn't know, what he can and can't do; a thorough
understanding of the subject and skill in communicating it
to the learner. One way around these shortcomings would be
to make the program 'learn'; in other words to be self-
adaptive as experience in use indicates the most successful
pathways and feedback loops. This, however, is beyond the
state of the art. The more familiar ways of using the
computer as a resource in the classroom are illustrated in
figure 2.

They do not depend upon the models which play such a
critical role when the machine is used as a surrogate
teacher. Here the computer acts as a resource on an equal
footing to, say, laboratory apparatus, to be used as and
when it has a part to play in providing or supporting
student enquiry. As long ago as 1969 the phrase, "What
would happen if . . . . . .?" was used to evoke the

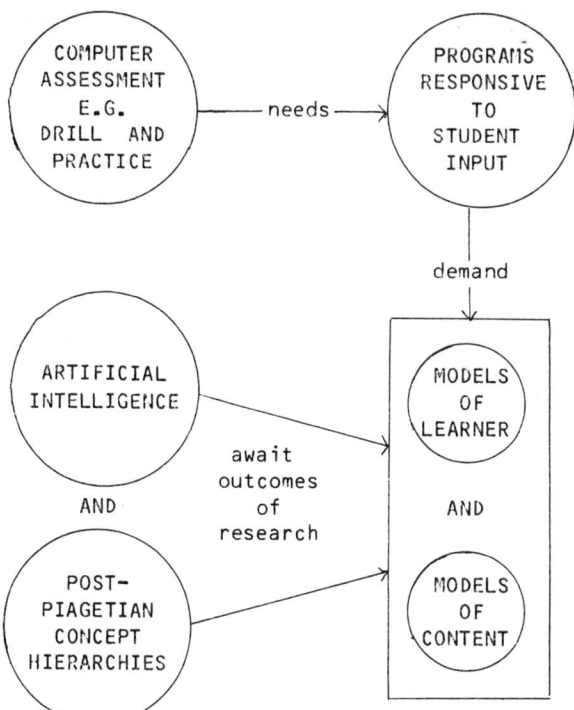

Figure 1. Computer in a predominantly didactic/teacher replacement role

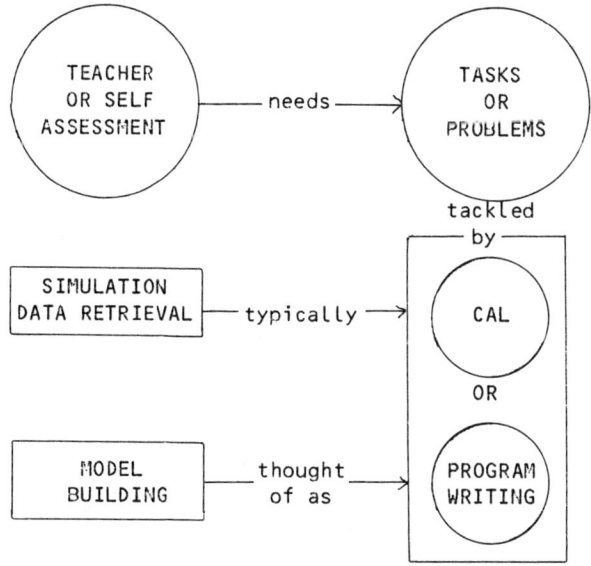

Figure 2. Computer in a resource role paralleled by laboratory investigation

43

pedagogical aims of the work at Chelsea. Ten years later
the 'happenings' relate not only to thought experiments in a
concrete universe but are also beginning to support the
abstractions of 'experimental mathematics'.

2. Designing a CAL unit

Although the title refers to 'programs', in the context of
this paper the computer programs cannot be considered in
isolation from other learning resources. Before turning to
the computer programs themselves and the way the new
microprocessor technology is affecting their detailed
design, it is important to consider the overall organisation
of a unit of CAL material, that is the way a topic is
approached when it is known that computer support is
available. A discussion of this, from choosing a topic to a
consideration of all items that make up an undergradute CAL
package, is given elsewhere [1]. For the purposes of this
paper some key points need to be high-lighted:
- (i) the CAL unit has to be related to other teaching
  resources and integrated with them when appropraite
- (ii) the CAL 'courseware' must communicate adequately
  the aims of the authors to, as yet inexperienced,
  teacher-users;
- (iii) even though a teacher may not wish to use prepared
  student material, at least it can convey very
  clearly the aims and experience of the authors;
- (iv) within the CAL unit printed material is important
  because it provides essential guidance;
- (v) material in a Socratic form provides a framework
  both for the author creating a unit and also for the
  student being led through the topic. Each question
  or problem forms part of a sequence which can become
  more open-ended as the topic becomes more familiar.
  This also offers more able students greater
  challenges.

2.1 A design case
The excerpt shown in figure 3, taken from a unit on
Satellite Orbits [2], illustrates the Socratic form.
Earlier questions reviewed the student's knowledge of the
independence of the perpendicular components of the motion
and the changing direction of the earth's gravitational
field. Now the question requires the student to apply his
knowledge to solve a more complex problem. At the time that
that unit was written and published, it would have been
unwise to expect that any school student would have access
to computer facilities more sophisticated than a teleprinter
terminal. So, the output shown in figure 4 is in the form
of a table of values. The form of the dialogue was

Q8 You know that for a body undergoing uniform acceleration $s = ut + \frac{1}{2}at^2$ (where s = distance, u = initial velocity, t = time and a = acceleration). Rearrange this relationship to get an expression for the time it takes a body to fall a distance, s, if it is dropped from rest.

Imagine an enormous flat table resting on one point of the earth's surface. Because the earth is round the ground gets further and further below the table as you move away from the point of contact. In fact by the time you have gone 6 km along the table the earth is about 3 m below you (Fig. 3). So if a body launched horizontally is going to go into orbit just above the earth's surface it must fall about 3 m in the time that it travels forward 6 km.

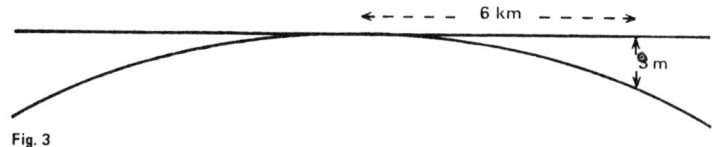

Fig. 3

Q9 Use you result to Q8 to calculate the time it will take the body to fall 3 m, with an acceleration of 10 m s^{-2}

Q10 How fast must the body be launched if it is to travel forward 6 km in this time?

Figure 3. Extract from the Student's Notes on Satellite Orbits

HEIGHT OF MOUNTAIN IN METRES? <u>10000</u>
STARTING SPEED IN METRES / SEC.? <u>8000</u>
PRINTOUT INTERVAL IN SECONDS? <u>300</u>

TIME (SECS)	HEIGHT (METRES)	SPEED (M/S)	ORBIT DEGREES
0	10000	8000	0
300	21700	7986	21.5
600	55200	7945	42.9
900	105600	7884	64
1200	166000	7812	84.7
1500	228500	7738	105.1

DO YOU WANT TO CONTINUE ?

Figure 4. Sample output from the program NEWTON (student's responses underlined)

correspondingly simple but that did not prevent the
questions in the Notes relating to the computer interaction
from being searching, as shown in figure 5.

Q11 What time is needed for an artificial satellite to go once around the earth?

Q12 What do you think happens to it after it returns to its starting point?

Q13 What happens to the orbit if the body is given a velocity slightly higher than is needed to
make it go into orbit?

Q14 At what point in the orbit does the body have (a) its maximum height (b) its minimum
height? What shape is the orbit?

Q15 From your answers to the last question you should be able to say where the body has
(a) its maximum (b) its minimum potential energy.

Q16 Once the body has been launched no engine or rocket on it is fired — so its total energy is
constant. Use this fact, and your answer to Q15 to say where the satellite *must* have
(a) most (b) least kinetic energy.

Figure 5. Further extract from the Student's Notes
on Satellite Orbits

3. Impact of the microcomputer on design

Now that it is possible (or rather practicable) to employ
diagrammatic or graphical displays in a CAL unit such as the
one described, there is a temptation to plot the satellite
path. But, it is important to ask what is gained by such a
change. The picture may be rather poor if a low resolution
display (roughly 80 x 60 addressable points on a screen) is
used, or quite acceptable if a higher resolution of 300 x
200 points, with or without colour, is available. In the
latter case the display as used in the special
implementation of NEWTON at the Science Museum's 'Challenge
of the Chip' exhibition can be eye-catching and motivating.

It is often the case, however, that a permanent paper record of the student's interaction is more important than a fleeting image on the screen. So, the Teacher's Guide to the unit suggested that, given tables of values, the students might well benefit from the activity of plotting the orbits for themselves on polar graph paper.

The last point is an example of one of the major dangers of increasingly clever machines. The unique charactersitic of CAL programs, when compared with film or television, is that the computer program demands a response from the students. The 'good' program encourages students to think before responding and presents students with information which is usable in the context of the task or problem with which they have been challenged. The Socratic form of the written material will be successful only if it provides a level of motivation through which the challenge of the problems is accepted by students. The associated programs must be in line with this strategy and leave students with tasks to perform. The 'clever' program which misuses the hardware facilities and leaves students with no decisions to make, or tasks to undertake, throws away the benefits of activity based learning; students mindlessly press buttons and make little progress in their understanding.

The key to sound pedagogical design of CAL materials lies in the careful structuring of students' activities. In the case of printed material, the structure takes the form of carefully selected set of questions or problems leads students up and over hurdles to their understanding. The problems must be solvable by the students and it is here that published material acts only as a guide for teachers in choosing the most appropriate set of hurdles for their own students. Having said that, it must also be acknowledged that well written materials, for which feedback from experienced teachers has been used as part of a formative evaluation, may well be suitable for quite a large number of students. In the case of a program, the structure relates rather to the quantity and quality of the information offered to students during their interaction. Having presented a table or a graph, it is important to be clear about what the student is expected to do with it. As shown earlier with the satellite orbit unit, a table can illustrate the attainment of a closed orbit. While a diagram may show this more vividly, it is a record of the entries in the table which is necessary if students are to explore, say, energy conservation through their own calculations on the table entries.

For each unit it is essential that the program is developed, paying particular attention to the form of output, alongside the questions proposed for the students' notes. When the only generally available terminals were those that printed on paper, which could only be fed in one direction, the choices for information display were limited. As the teleprinter was likely to be slow, instructions and other text had to be kept to a minimum to reduce boredom (and cost). So the unit was structured around the attainable form of interaction. There is more than a grain of truth in the belief that these restrictions led to a discrimination in the use of computers and in the form of dialogue, which has been a valuable experience.

At the moment a very interesting exercise is underway because funds are available for the production of second editions of all the secondary level science materials published under the Chelsea Sciences Simulation Project and the Schools Council Project 'Computers in the Curriculum'. These teleprinter orientated materials are being reviewed for re-publication. Use will be made of the displays available on the best of the current microcomputer systems, though it has been judged that colour should not be used. This work has again thrown the authors into the centre of the kind of considerations previously outlined. Some units are seen to be adequately served by a purely alphanumeric interaction. These are situations in which the CAL unit is used in parallel with a laboratory or paper and pencil task and there is a clear benefit in emphasising the correspondence between the two activities. Also there is serious concern about the role of a permanent paper record. It cannot be assumed that screen images on paper can be obtained easily or at reasonable cost by the students involved. However, it may well be that the past dominance of the teleprinter has led to an overdependence on a paper record and that this has meant the under-valuing of skills in undertaking real investigations and observations. These skills include deciding what information is going to be useful to solve the problem in hand and hence in making a careful record of the relevant observations.

The 'paper record vs. visual display' issue is but one of many issues. Information can be built up on the screen over some time period and it can be alphanumeric data, graphs and diagrams all with highlighting or colour. Over the years the techniques of presenting good static pictures and diagrams to support text have been perfected (perhaps too strong a word) by publishers and by advertisers. The messages from Rolls Royce, Guinness and White Horse come over clearly. Dynamic pictures and diagrams have also been skillfully employed on film and through television. But microcomputers are now opening a quite new dimension – that of interactive dynamic display.

4. Building displays

Now, the design of programs has to take into account the
students' interactions as they modify features of a dynamic
display. Key features include the amount of information
changed and the speed of that change. In preparing a static
illustration an essential consideration is the amount of
information displayed. In preparing a film, the amount and
rate of addition or subtraction of information is under the
designer's control. But with computer displays, the
designer has also to consider how a student's actions affect
the amount and rate of change of information. It is
necessary to consider:

> the rate at which information is displayed;
> the option for student control over this rate;
> the quanta of new information displayed between
> student reponses;
> the ease of identification of each quanta;
> the total amount of information displayed on the
> screen at any time;
> the loss of information and ability to recall;
> the form of information (number, word, diagram, etc.);
> the method of student response.

As much as possible, the student or teacher should be
allowed control over the factors. This applies to direct
student use of programs and equally (and perhaps more easily
attainably) to teacher use in class tutorial or 'electronic
blackboard' mode.

At the moment there is rather little experience or substance
in research findings for a program designer to call upon to
help him make the decisions. There seeems to be no direct
way of making use of the commercial skills of advertising
agencies. Such skills could produce new display and
interaction forms. In this new research, each of the display
factors needs to be examined taking care to isolate it from
the rest. The starting point should be firmly linked to a
consideration of what information a student requires at each
point in the interaction. In other words, what specific
question is the student trying to answer, and so how should
helpful information be presented?

Leaving aside for a moment the form of the display, there is
another important but independent program design issue. This
relates to the form of the dialogue. In most of the earlier
Chelsea schools material, the student was guided (some might
critically say, confined) by a dialogue structured in a way
meant to be supportive and to some extent influenced by the
kind of investigations it was anticipated that a student
would wish to undertake. An alternative is to offer a much
more open student choice through a series of options chosen
by keywords or codes. This was used in our undergraduate
projects, mainly to save space on an already overcrowded

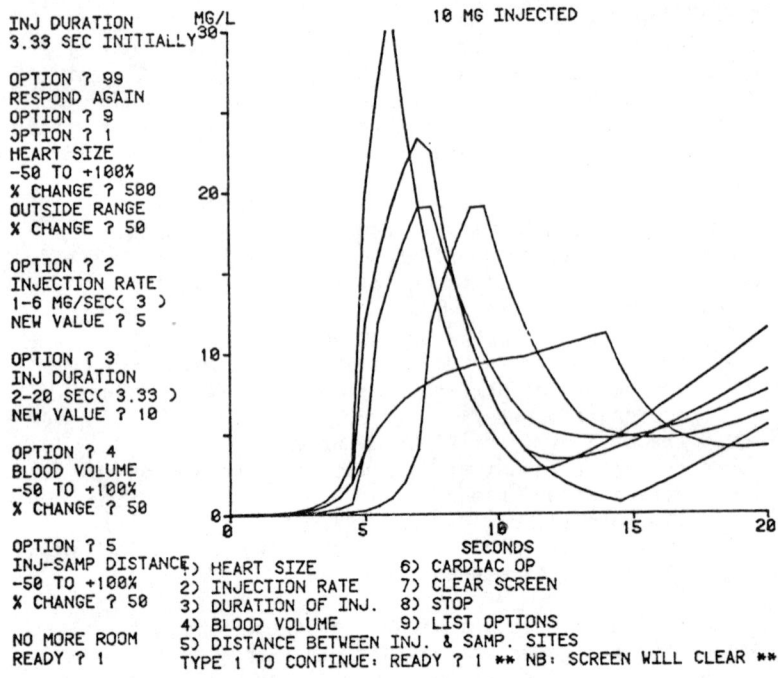

```
INJ DURATION        MG/L              10 MG INJECTED
3.33 SEC INITIALLY  30

OPTION ? 99
RESPOND AGAIN
OPTION ? 9
OPTION ? 1
HEART SIZE
-50 TO +100%
X CHANGE ? 500      20
OUTSIDE RANGE
X CHANGE ? 50

OPTION ? 2
INJECTION RATE
1-6 MG/SEC( 3 )
NEW VALUE ? 5

OPTION ? 3          10
INJ DURATION
2-20 SEC( 3.33 )
NEW VALUE ? 10

OPTION ? 4
BLOOD VOLUME
-50 TO +100%
X CHANGE ? 50        0
OPTION ? 5            0        5         10        15       20
INJ-SAMP DISTANCE 1) HEART SIZE        SECONDS
-50 TO +100%      2) INJECTION RATE    6) CARDIAC OP
X CHANGE ? 50     3) DURATION OF INJ.  7) CLEAR SCREEN
                  4) BLOOD VOLUME      8) STOP
NO MORE ROOM      5) DISTANCE BETWEEN INJ. & SAMP. SITES
READY ? 1         TYPE 1 TO CONTINUE: READY ? 1 ** NB: SCREEN WILL CLEAR **
```

Figure 6. Graphics screen after student use of an
          undergraduate unit on cardiac output. Too much
          information for a static picture but perhaps
          acceptable due to gradual build-up

graphics screen, and by the Home Heating unit [3] because of
the large number of parameters available for student
control. In that case, all parameters had default values and
the status of the house design could be requested at any
time by using one of the keywords. So, a number of special

50

keywords were defined which set in train alternative
dialogues, each aimed to assist with a certain set of
problems. Going a step beyond this, the new programs not
only give authors the flexibility of dialogue structure but
easily allow a teacher to define new dialogue if he believes
that it would be more appropriate for particular students.
Complete freedom of action may be suitable for able students
but the loss of guidance when the dialogue is removed could
prove to be serious for the majority. The new structure
should allow flexibility in moving from one style to
another.

5. Conclusion

Only a few of the design isssues facing authors have been
discussed. With the rapid change in technology certain to
continue, it is important to view them critically and
flexibly. If this paper were to be written in several years
time it might well be dealing with issues in the use of
speech circuits and video disks. Clearly, though, we must be
wary of being stampeded into design changes in order to keep
up with the technology. A fairly short term pragmatic
approach to advances is necessary — but this will be fairly
safe as long as practising teachers play a major part in the
developments.

References

1. R.LEWIS and P.J.MURPHY, Product Design and Development,
   in Interactive Computer Graphics in Sciance Teaching,
   eds. Mackenzie Elton and Lewis, Ellis Horwood, 1978

2. J.HARRIS, NEWTON - unit on satellite orbits, Chelsea
   Science Simulation Project, Edward Arnold, 1975

3. R.D.MASTERTON and R.LEWIS (eds), Computers in the
   Curriculum - Home Heating, Schools Council / Edward
   Arnold, 1979

GRAPHICAL DESIGN
OF TEACHING SIMULATIONS

P.R.Smith and C.Blandford

Computer Assisted Teaching Unit
Queen Mary College
Mile End Road
London E1 4NS

1. Introduction

The role of computer based simulation in education has been
discussed at length elsewhere ([1],[2]) and will not be
elaborated in this paper, which is concerned with the way in
which computer graphics can be used to good effect in such
teaching simulations. The experience upon which these
remarks is based extends over almost a decade during which
graphical display has been used as an integral part of
computer based teaching procedures; the field of application
has been engineering, at tertiary level, with emphasis on
electrical and nuclear engineering. Each simulation program
has within it a model of an engineering system, so devised
that the student may investigate its properties and
responses and, in so doing, consolidate and extend the
knowledge which he has gained from lectures, tutorials or
laboratories. The computer based learning element is seen as
a complementary component of the learning process offering,
in addition, a range of experience of engineering systems
which would not otherwise be available to the student.

The effective use of teaching simulations demands an
interactive computing environment with rapid response at the
terminal. The examples which are used in illustration are
all taken from computer based learning material which has
been devised for and implemented on a multi-user minicomputer system; the single user micro-computer can equally
provide the required interaction and response, although the
current quality of graphical display often leaves something
to be desired. Many aspects of the use of graphics discussed
below will be immediately relevant to micro-computer
systems, whilst others can be seen as indicative of the
quality of graphical display which is desirable.

Graphical display introduces a new dimension into the use of
teaching simulations. Engineering undergraduates are
accustomed to the graphical display of information and would
in many cases, be obliged to plot the results of their
computations if these were presented in tabular form, in
order to extract relevant information. But there are also
advantages less tangible than increased speed of

assimilation; these relate to the improved quality of the
learning experience when graphical display is usd both for
input and output of data. There is ample qualitative
evidence of this improvement, from the observations of
teachers and from the comments of students in response to
questionnaires and in individual interviews.

2. Structure of a teaching simulation

The structure of a computer based teaching simulation, shown
in figure 1, is deceptively simple, comprising four areas
dealing respectively with the initialisation of the model,
the computation of results, the display of results and the

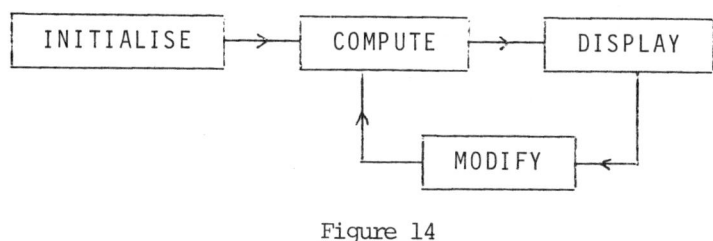

Figure 14

modification of the model for the next computation.
Initialisation is concerned with setting the parametric
values required to allow computation to proceed and a number
of decisions have to be made before the associated routines
can be written. In many simulations there will be both fixed
and variable input parameters, which determine a particular
realisation of a general model, and variable parameters
whose values, or ranges of values, are to be set by the
student when the program is run. Decisions have to be taken
at an early stage as to which parameters are to be variable
and whether the program is to offer single or multiple
calculation runs. Data should be checked on entry to avoid
program failure due to unacceptable value or type matching
and the completed data set should be available for display
and correction.

The need for validation of input data can be combined with
provision for free format data entry in a subroutine which
replaces the conventional input statement. Languages for
scientific programming offer little in the way of input
validation to exclude data values which will cause the
program to fail, but in a computer based teaching program
not only must such failures be excluded but also informative

53

messages must be provided at the terminal when interception occurs.

Graphical display can be used to present input procedures in a form attractive to the user, and in some instances can provide an effective means of checking that the input data is correct. This is particulary applicable to simulations involving networks where correct connectivity can readily be established by the display of a diagram of the circuit defined by the input data.

The computation subroutines are usually straightforward and present no special problems if the calculation has been properly specified. In some engineering simulations the computation time may become large enough to require periodic activation of the terminal to reassure the user that computation is still proceeding. A useful stratagem using graphical display is to generate a pattern on the screen in step with the calculation, as a progress indicator.

It is in the display of the results of computation that graphics has most to offer, and this will be discussed in more detail below. The characteristics of a particular graphical display terminal will influence the way it is used: the selective erase facility of refresh graphics cannot be replicated on a storage tube device; the size of the addressable screen matrix will influence the amount of information which can be displayed; the availability of cursor or light pen will affect the design of the user interaction. Most of the illustrative examples in this paper are taken from programs using Tektronix 4010 storage tube graphics terminals and high level routines compatible with the GINO drawing system [3]. These programs can be implemented on Tektronix-compatible refresh systems without modification, provided that a GINO library of drawing routines is available; a kernel of 20 graphics routines has been found to be adequate for most simulations. The deliberate exclusion of some attractive features of graphical display systems from the programs has resulted in a product which ought to be readily transferrable from one type of machine to another, and this is desirable if the considerable development costs associated with computer based learning programs are to be held to a reasonable level.

The requirements for display will be very dependent upon the characteristics of the particular simulation. In one it will be adequate to show the variation of a single parameter, in another a family of graphs may be needed; a single pass calculation may be adequate, or it may be necessary to retain data for eventual comparative display after a number of passes. Hard copy is usually required at some stage in a teaching simulation and the relation of this provision to

the display procedures needs careful thought. Data from
which the display can be redrawn can be directed to a
printing device or the screen content can be reproduced on a
plotter or hard copy device. The choice of one or more of
these alternatives will depend upon the characteristics of
an individual simulation.

The final section of the program allows the user, having
viewed the results of the current computation, to redefine
the system in pursuit of the objectives of his study. This
usually features the use of 'menus' or option lists, which
should be carefully structured to facilitate the
modifications appropriate to the problem without unnecessary
data redefinition which can be destructive of user interest.
The optimum set of options may not become apparent until
experience has been gained through use of the program by
students. It is sometimes advantageous to display the option
set alongside the current results, so that a choice can be
made with all pertinent information in view; this has the
disadvantage, however, of reducing the area of screen
available for the display of results. In a typical multi-
variate engineering system where ranges of several
parameters are being investigated, it may be appropriate to
reset initial values at the end of a run or to retain the
current data set; whichever procedure is adopted, it must be
made clear to the user.

The criteria for decomposition of a program into modules
must be given careful thought at an early stage in the
design, and this is especially true when graphical display
is used extensively. Features which are specific to a
particular computer or operating system, or to a particular
graphics terminal, should be avoided if possible. If their
use is essential they should be isolated in clearly
indicated modules with the objective that changes which
become necessary on transfer to another system are
restricted to these modules.

3. The role of graphical display

The areas of use of computer graphics in teaching
simulations can be identified as :-
    display of introductory text with illustrative diagrams
    display of circuit, nodal or descriptive diagrams
    related to a realisation of a system defined by the user
    display of results in the form of graphs or diagrams
    display of designs or diagrams to indicate the progress
    of computation
In addition, once graphical display is available, it may be
used to control data input, verification and validation.

In view of the complementary nature of the teaching role of

simulation programs, the display of introductory material
might be seen as merely cosmetic, since the user can be
assumed to be familiar with the embodied model when he
begins to use the program. Experience has shown, however,
that it is useful to offer a reminder of some of the salient
features of the model to introduce the user to the
simulation, at the same time pointing out some of the
details of the structure of the program which he may need to
know. This is illustrated in figure 2, a display from a

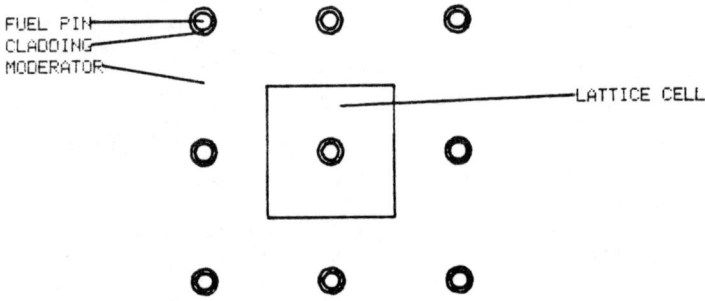

A COMPUTER EXPERIMENT IN REACTOR PHYSICS

NEUTRON MULTIPLICATION IN A FUEL-MODERATOR LATTICE

A FOUR-FACTOR FORMULA MODEL OF THE NEUTRON CYCLE IS

USED TO CALCULATE THE INFINITE MULTIPLICATION FACTOR

FOR A SQUARE LATTICE OF CLAD CYLINDRICAL FUEL PINS

SEPARATED BY A MODERATOR.

FUEL PIN
CLADDING
MODERATOR

LATTICE CELL

SECTION OF THE LATTICE, SHOWING LATTICE CELL

Figure 2. Display of introductory text and diagram
from a program which examines neutron
multiplication in a nuclear reactor lattice

program examining neutron multiplication. There will also
be examples where lectures and tutorials have dealt with the
general properties of a system while the computer simulation
refers to a specific realisation, details of which need to
be supplied. A typical example is the electrical
distribution system shown in figure 3. Examples of systems
defined by the user can be found in many engineering
applications, in particular where network analysis is
required. For example, figure 4 displays a network with a
nodal structure. It was defined by the user in a sequence of
input tables, one of which is shown in Figure 5. Here the

56

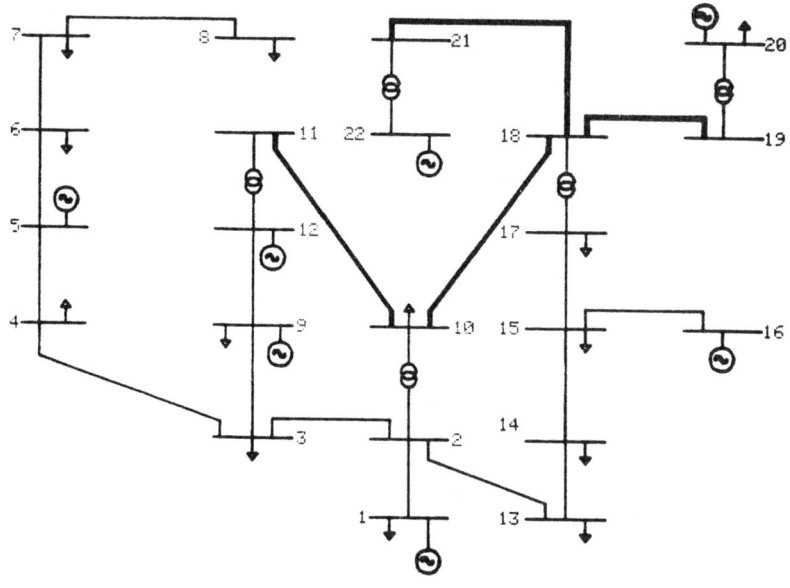

Figure 3. Display of a pre-set electrical
distribution system

diagram helps the user to check that the network has been
correctly entered, a route being provided for data
modification if it has not. Tabular data entry may, at first
sight, appear rather cumbersome and it certainly requires
considerable programming effort to take account of the
increased significance of the position of characters on the
screen. It does, however, allow the eye to scan quickly
through the data to check irregularities or inconsistencies,
and the combination with a diagrammatic display can be a
most effective method of executing otherwise tedious data
input. Nodes of a network and their connectivity may be
used to describe many engineering systems - for example an
electric circuit, an electrical distribution network, a
two-dimensional pin-jointed truss or a pipe layout. The use
of tabular input is an alternative to the use of device
dependent features such as light pen and cursor. These
devices can be used to specify the nodal layout by direct
entry to the screen, but their use may lead to the
introduction of positional errors and to problems of program
transfer. In some programs, for some elements of input data,

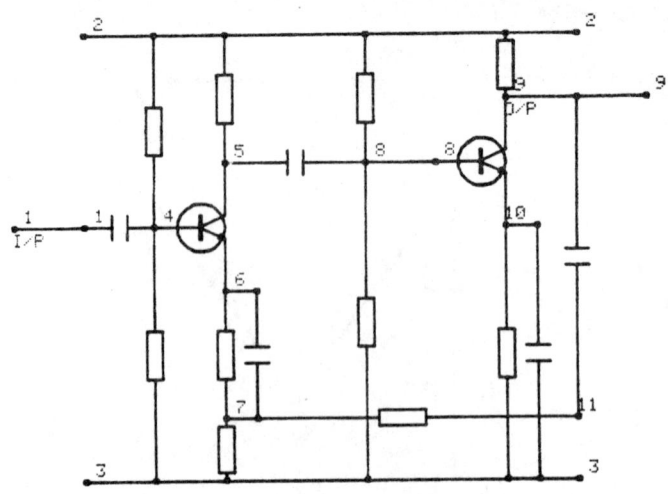

Figure 4. Display of an electrical circuit from a
program which investigates frequency response

TABLE FOR PASSIVE BRANCHES

NODE 1	NODE 2	R (K)	C (PF)	L (UH)
1	4		.1000E+08	
2	4	56.00		
4	3	27.00		
2	5	2.70		
6	7	2.70	.5000E+08	
7	3	0.03		
5	8		.1000E+08	
2	8	56.00		
8	3	27.00		
2	9	2.70		
10	3	2.70	.5000E+08	
9	11		.1000E+09	
11	7	6.80		

Figure 5. Tabular data entry associated with the
circuit shown in figure 3

it is difficult to avoid the use of such devices; for
example, in prescribing the layout of the electrical

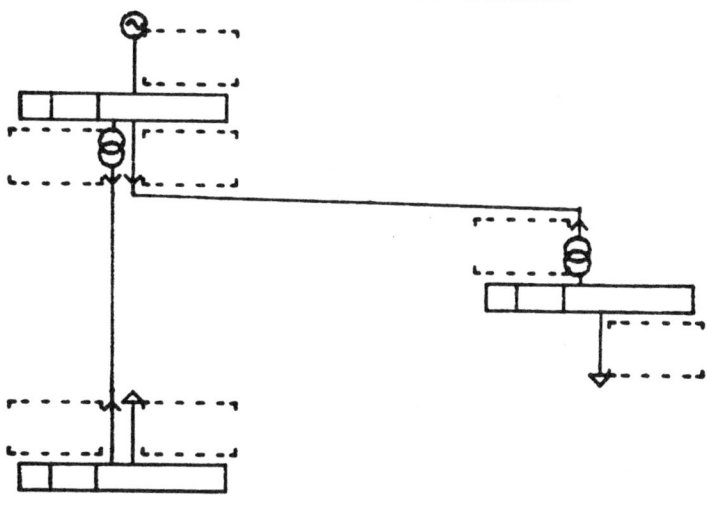

Figure 6. Display from the procedures for setting
up an electrical distribution network
prescribed by the user

distribution network shown in figure 6. Ideally the
instructions required by the user should appear on the
screen as part of the current display so that he can proceed
without needing to refer to documentation or recalling
information presented earlier in the program. This is
illustrated by the display in figure 7 which tells the user
how to complete the table of values. Special user languages
should be avoided unless essential. There is little merit in
using abbreviated prompts (e.g. R?) when a full request in
plain English (e.g. ENTER RESISTANCE IN OHMS) can be
displayed more quickly than it can be read. It may be
effective to display both data and diagram at the same time.

The third area in which graphical display can be put to good
use is the obvious one of presenting results in the form of
graphs or diagrams. The usual procedure using storage tube
graphics is to generate all the numbers to be plotted and
then offer them to a scaling routine which will draw and
label suitable axes and plot the graph. The graph should be
identified, preferably by a heading rather than by
attempting to write labels in the limited space usually

LOADING TABLE

JOINT NUMBER	MAGNITUDE OF LOAD	ORIENTATION TO THE HORIZONTAL	
7 7	1.000E+01 100	-90.000 H	JOINT REDEFINED

TYPE H FOR HORIZONTAL ORIENTATION

      U FOR VERTICAL ORIENTATION

OTHERWISE TYPE THE ANGLE

CHANGE A LINE OF DATA BY RETYPING THE LINE

TYPE F TO FINISH INPUT

TYPE E TO EXIT TO OPTION LIST

Figure 7. Routine to specify the loading of
a pin jointed truss, showing user
instructions

available on the axes. An example of output of a single
graph is shown in figure 8. When the user has examined the
graph, he may wish to display other system parameters, if
appropriate, and he may wish to retain or discard the
current data set.

Figure 9 illustrates the display of current output combined
with an option list which offers these facilities. If option
2 is selected and previous results are already stored, the
user is immediately offered the option of a comparative
display. When multiple graphs are displayed, care should be
taken not to exceed a useful density of information; usually
not more than 5 or 6 graphs should be superimposed. Each
graph must be labelled with an identifier, and a key to the
identifiers must be displayed on the screen beside the
graphs as shown in figure 10. This may be difficult if
several data items need to be specified to identify a set of
results. In other situations, it may be necessary to provide
the user with a key in printed form, merely labelling the
data sets on the screen as SET1, SET2, etc. This is
illustrated in figure 11.

60

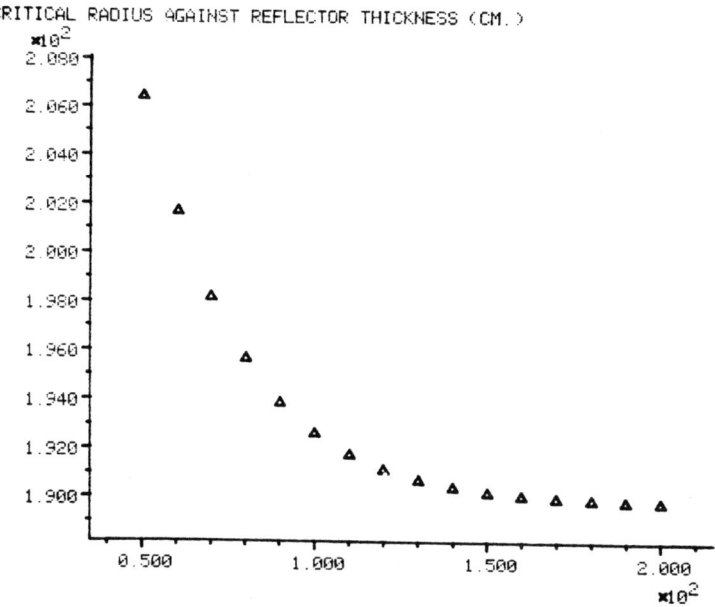

Figure 8. A simpe example of graph plotting
to show the variation of critical
radius of a spherical nuclear reactor
with reflector thickness

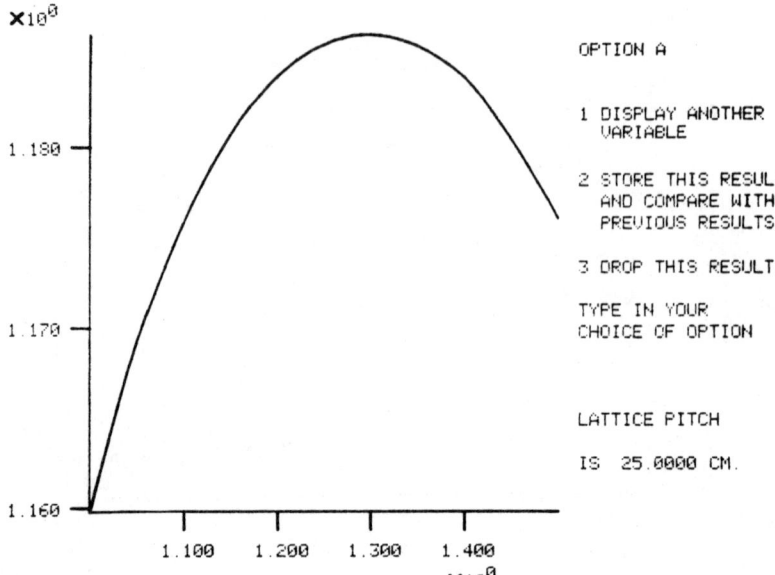

Figure 9. Combined graph and option list from
a program investigating neutron
multiplication in a nuclear reactor
lattice

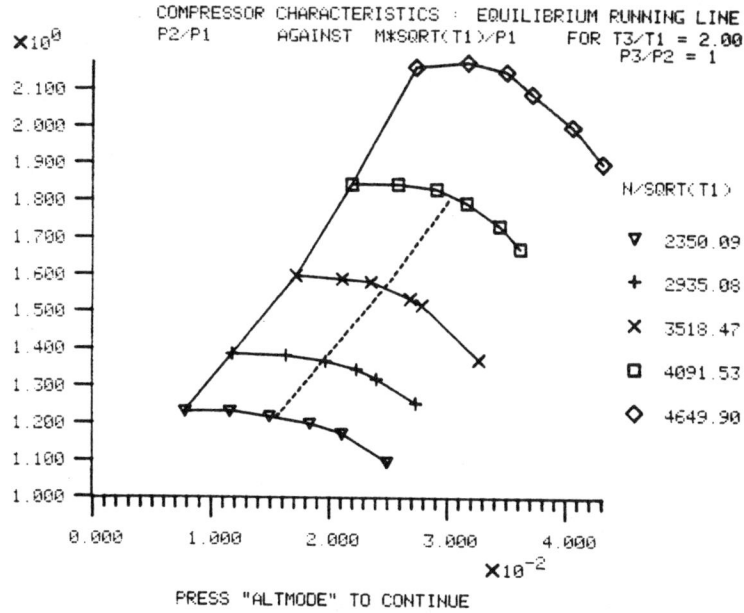

Figure 10. An example of a multiple graph with key
from a program modelling a turbo-charger

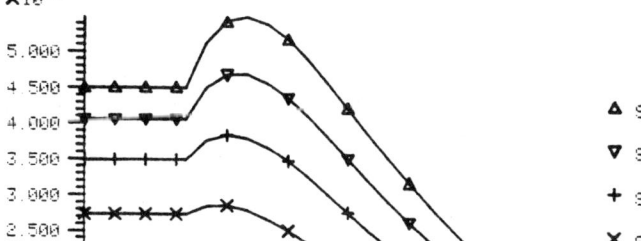

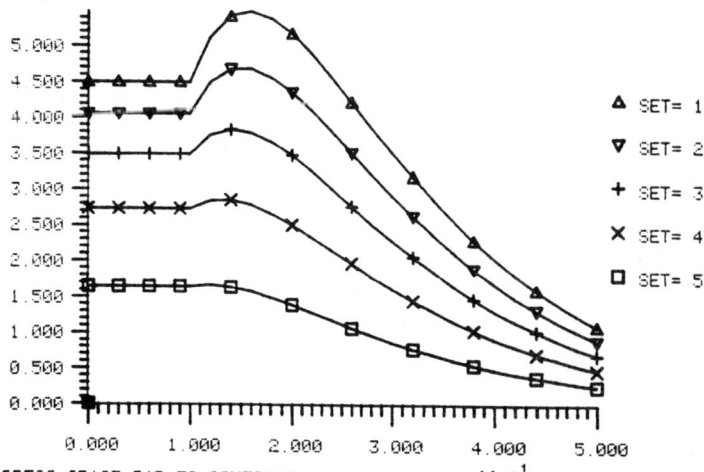

Figure 11. Multiple graph from a program investigating
xenon transients in a nuclear reactor

Since there will always be a limit to the number of data
sets which can be stored, a 'save or discard' routine must
be offered after each multiple graph display. A generalised
flow diagram to give the various facilities which have been

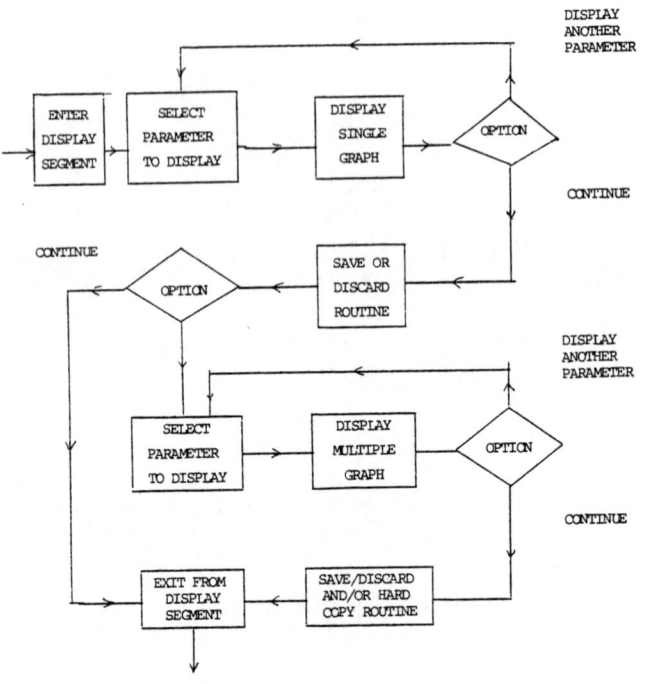

Figure 12. Flow diagram from the display
section of a simulation

described is shown in figure 12. The graphical display of
results is not always the most effective form of
presentation; for example, it may be more informative, in
the analysis of a network, to superimpose results upon the
network diagram itself. In figure 13 values are superimposed
on the network diagram shown in figure 3. In other
applications a tabular presentation of results together with
an informative diagram may be more effective. This
combination is illustrated in figure 14. In this program,
which analyses a pin-jointed truss, the user has assessed
the state of stress of each member of the truss and is here
able to judge the accuracy of that assessment.

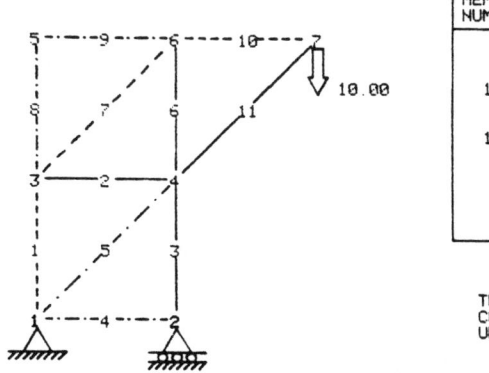

MEMBER FORCE TABLE

MEMBER NUMBER	FORCE	ASSESSMENT
4	0.0000E-01	U
2	-1.0000E+01	C
9	0.0000E-01	U
10	1.0000E+01	T
5	0.0000E-01	U
7	1.4142E+01	T
11	-1.4142E+01	C
1	1.0000E+01	T
8	0.0000E-01	U
3	-2.0000E+01	C
6	-1.0000E+01	C

KEY

TENSION	– – – –
COMPRESSION	————
UNSTRESSED	– · — · –

PRESS RETURN TO DISPLAY REACTIONS

TYPE F TO FINISH DISPLAYING RESULTS

TYPE E TO EXIT TO OPTION LIST

Figure 13. Distribution network with superimposed results
In other applications a tabular presentation
of results together with an informative diagram
may be more effective (figure 14)

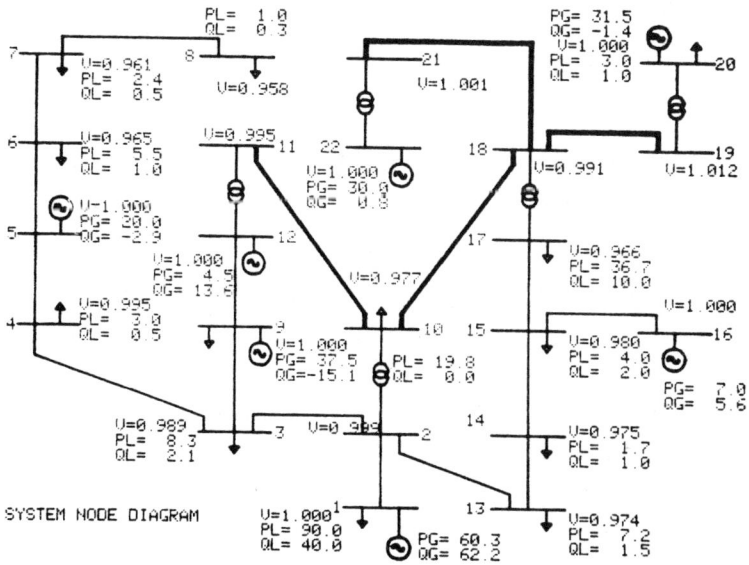

Figure 14. Tabular presentation of results combined with
informative diagram, from pin jointed truss
analysis program

65

Finally, graphical display can be utilised to keep the user informed and happy during a lengthy computation. This is not a trivial matter; experience shows that undergraduates rapidly become anxious or bored if the terminal shows no response, this setting in after as little as five or ten seconds. The psychological effect upon the learning process, whilst hard to quantify, is readily apparent. (The effect upon the terminal, which is subjected to much key prodding, takes longer to appear). If the computation proceeds in a step by step fashion it may be possible to output intermediate results at the terminal at each step; indeed, this may have educational value, for example, in a finite difference analysis, illustrated in figure 15, where such

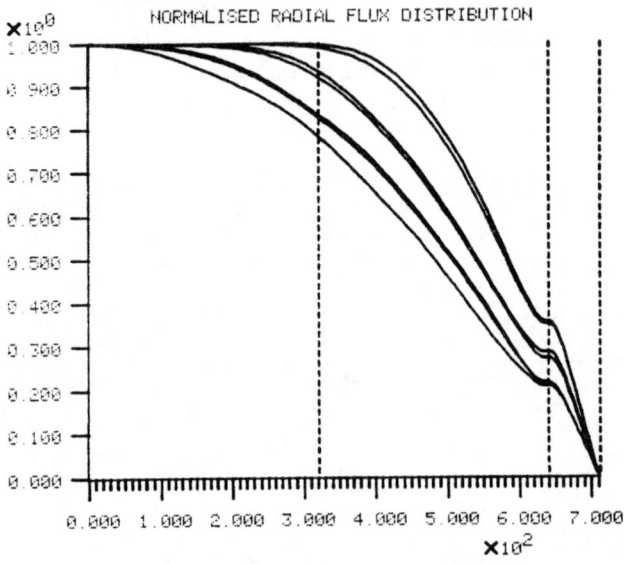

Figure 15. Display showing the progress of convergence in a finite difference calculation of a neutron distribution

results give an indication of the process of convergence. Even if no such useful information can be extracted, the terminal should still be activated at pre-set intervals, for example, using a random pattern generator which can be organised to complete a pattern in synchronisation with the completion of the calculation.

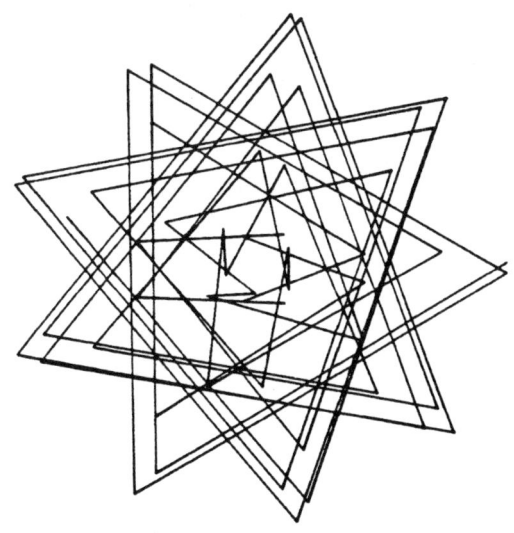

Figure 16. An example of random pattern generation

4. Concluding remarks

The effectiveness of a computer based simulation as an
educational tool is enhanced by the use of graphical
display. In the design of the computer program which
embodies the simulation, careful thought has to be given at
an early stage to the precise way in which graphical display
is to be used. Some of the considerations have been
discussed in this paper. Experience at Queen Mary College
over a number of years has convinced the authors that the
additional effort required in implementation is well
justified by the attractiveness of the graphics-based
simulations. Whilst many low cost micro-computer systems are
at present unable to offer the high definition graphics
capability from which the illustrative examples have
derived, the general principles discussed are none-the-less
relevant to micro-computer applications.

References

1. COUNCIL for EDUCATIONAL TECHNOLOGY, Computer Assisted
   Learning in Higher Education — the next ten years,
   Technical Report no. 14, 1977.

2. D.A.TAWNEY (ed.), Learning Through Computers, Macmillan
   Press Ltd., 1979.

3. GINO-F general purpose graphics package: User's Manual,
   C.A.D. Centre, Madingley Road, Cambridge.

RE-LEARNING MATHEMATICS THROUGH LOGO: HELPING STUDENT TEACHERS WHO DON'T UNDERSTAND MATHEMATICS

Benedict du Boulay

Department of Computer Science, University of Aberdeen

and

Jim Howe

Department of Artificial Intelligence
University of Edinburgh

1. Introduction

Teaching mathematics is never an easy task. It is especially difficult when one is dealing with students who are training to be primary school teachers and who are finding mathematics troublesome and unpleasant. The problem is compounded by the fact that these students may have had a history of mathematical failure which now, at a late stage in their education, desperately needs to be put right. There have been attempts to exclude these students from teacher training courses by raising College entry qualifications in mathematics, but to little avail since the possession of an '0' grade (or '0' level) pass in mathematics is not a particularly reliable predictor of competence to teach primary school mathematics. Given that the problem cannot be side-stepped, a search of the literature in mathematics teaching reveals little of value written about helping student teachers once they are in college.

We have been investigating the value of providing mathematically weak students with computer based facilities for carrying out mathematical experiments on troublesome topics by writing and/or running computer programs written in LOGO. LOGO is a general purpose interactive programming language that has been designed for use by programming novices. It has many features to make both programming and mathematics fun to learn. For instance, most implementations enable the student to control a drawing device called a Turtle which can be made to produce mathematically interesting and visually pleasing shapes. The Turtle itself is a small motorised cart equipped with a pen that moves under program control. The Turtle is often simulated as a spot of light on a display screen to provide faster and more accurate diagrams. LOGO can also manipulate symbolic data in the form of numbers, words or lists. LOGO makes it simple to define, debug, edit and store new procedures which can be used as "building blocks" in complex programs. This latter feature together with its ability to draw allow the new programmer to produce an interesting working program very quickly after sitting down at a terminal for the first time. To explore topics in mathematics, the student usually needs access to the appropriate "kit of mathematical parts". LOGO is an ideal "kit-building" language due to the ease with which new procedures can be defined to make up, for example, geometry systems, set manipulating systems and so on.

The pedagogical rationale behind this LOGO-based approach is, first, that the activity is fun and intriguing and should break down the student's negative attitude to the subject. Second, writing a computer program about a mathematical topic forces the student to confront that topic and her understanding of it. Third, use of the computer's graphic capability provides a visual, and possibly dynamic, illustration of a topic that the student might otherwise find hard to visualise. For example, a student who has trouble visualising multiplication of fractions can run a program that illustrates this idea in a series of diagrams, seeing how that program behaves with fractions of her own choice.

In principle, the approach has much to offer but as ever in education its practice has highlighted a number of areas where tradeoffs have to be made. One of these is between the sense of involvement and personal discovery associated with writing programs and the investment of scarce time in learning the necessary programming skills. Another tradeoff is between the power, freedom and complexity of using a general purpose language, like LOGO, and the simplicity but constraints of using pre-defined programs or a "kit" specially developed for a particular topic.

In addition to the tradeoffs, a number of hard problems face those who wish to help student teachers of low mathematical attainment. There is the basic problem that the mathematical understanding of the student can be even poorer than the scores in tests of mathematical performance suggest. For some students there is the problem of persuading them to acknowledge that they need mathematical help, while for others there is the problem of overcoming their pessimism and fatalism about their mathematical inability. In both these cases, factors within the College of Education can help or hinder the effectiveness of computer-based remedial help.

Within the computer-based course itself there are the problems of choosing an appropriate programming language (or implementing suitable maths procedures), designing effective remedial teaching activities, working with the available computing facilities and negotiating institutional constraints such as limits on the time available for computer-based work due to the intrusion of lengthy periods of teaching practice, College exams and so on.

This all sound rather negative. But the results of two evaluative studies which we have carried out show that these problems can be substantially overcome and that the approach has some success in both improving students' attitudes to mathematics and their understanding of mathematics [2], [3].

2. Test performance and classroom teaching

Results from studies carried out be Rees [8] and by Lumb [4] into the mathematical test performance of student teachers are depressing. Rees has identified a 'common core' of concepts that seem to be misunderstood by many student teachers, and our work using Rees' test supports this [1]. For example, students made mistakes with decimals and with square roots, and were not able to calculate the square root of 0.9 correctly. Lumb showed that many students made errors in what ought to have been simple tasks, such as dividing one decimal by another, and that even after their mathematics course there were still 53% who made the same kind of error. He also showed that even some students with '0' level mathematics performed poorly. Lumb commented that "the depth of ignorance of mathematical facts and basic computation skills revealed in the initial test were absolutely staggering."

If one goes into the classroom and observes the student teacher at work on teaching practice, the situation can look even worse. The student may have sufficient knowledge to perform adequately in a mathematical test but still not have the understanding to teach effectively or to help pupils who do not understand. For instance, certain concepts in elementary arithmetic are notoriously difficult to teach e.g. multiplication of negative integers or dividing by a fraction. That is to say, it is hard to explain just why the rules for manipulating the notation are sensible, though of course it is easy enough to assert simply that they must be followed.

Even innocent looking topics like simple division can cause enormous difficulties. For example it is important for the teacher to distinguish, at least in her own mind, between division considered as sharing and division considered as partitioning. Both are represented by a division sum, say 15/5, but each is treating division in a different way. Each also needs a different manipulation of concrete apparatus to illustrate it. Considered as sharing, 15/5 would mean distribute 15 objects equally among 5 people, while considered as partitioning it would mean find out how many bundles of 5 objects can be taken from 15 objects. When the teacher does not understand the difference between these two, even though she can 'do' division herself, the words she uses to explain division and the terms she uses to describe what to do with apparatus can confuse her pupils. For instance, if pupils are given counters to help them understand division, in one case, having shared out the counters among 5 recipients, the child should count the number of counters in each share, and in the other case, having partitioned the counters into groups of 5 each, he should count up the number of groups. But if the teacher draws his attention to groups of counters when she has given the task of sharing, she can cause him to answer that 15/5 is 5 rather than 3. Conversely, if she talks about numbers of counters in the context of partitioning, he is quite likely to give a similar wrong answer.

Other cases that we have observed include a student who described "14 - 3" as "fourteen from three". She based this on a literal translation of "-" as "from". She could do subtraction sums herself correctly but was confused about the language to be employed in referring to expressions involving subtraction. Lumb [4] also found a small number of students who believed subtraction was commutative i.e. the operands for "-" could be put in either order without changing the value of the expression.

Students have various strategies for coping with difficult mathematical topics on teaching practice. They can usually arrange to be doing something mathematically undemanding when observed by their tutors. In other cases, if the children do raise difficult problems they can, in the words of one of our experimental subjects, "fob them off with something else".

3. The college of education
Once the College has identified a particular student as having mathematical difficulty it must decide what action to take. Students, like other people, are sensitive to being singled out as exceptions. They take even greater exception to being labelled "remedial", and so care has to be exercised not only in devising what these students should do but also in choosing what their activity shoud be called. Students are obviously interested in the criteria by which they have been judged to need mathematical help and react badly to a coarse classification based solely on marks gained in an examination if they are only just on the wrong side of the borderline.

Our observation of classes designed to help students in difficulty has found two distinct approaches which have repercussions for the introduction of the computer based methods that we advocate. In one approach the fact that the students in the class have been judged to need mathematical help is never publicly and explicitly stated during meetings of that class. Discussion about a tricky mathematical topic, such as fractions, is related to the difficulties which may face the future pupils of the student teachers, but not to the present difficulties of the student teachers with that topic. In private, both the lecturer and the students may readily admit that the students are finding fractions hard, but this is not frankly acknowledged between the two parties. It leads to an unreal teaching situation where each side talks about children's difficulties where they actually mean student's difficulties. Introducing computer-based methods that demand honesty about one's difficulties clashes with the above approach.

The advantage of this approach is that it does not obviously undermine the students' self-respect (by questioning their ability to understand primary school mathematics) and it does enable a traditionally full course of work to be covered because it makes little provision for re-teaching the elementary mathematics. But it can leave the student very frustrated because the unwritten classroom rules preclude the student asking the basic questions which trouble her, and so the opportunity for her to re-learn her mathematics can be lost.

The other approach accepts and acknowledges the students' difficulties and is a more congenial context into which to introduce computer-based methods. The students' activities are geared as much to their own difficulties as to those of their future pupils. It has the advantage that it makes it legitimate for the student to indicate the ideas that she does not understand, in the hope that something can be done about them. Though whichever approach is adopted, there will always be a certain amount of pressure on the student to hide her weaknesses for fear that revealing them may prejudice her Diploma.

The disadvantages of the open approach are that the subsequent re-exploration of mathematics can be very time-consuming and it is hard to conduct satisfactorily. There are various reasons for this difficulty. Some students may have disliked and been confused by mathematics for a long time and may have little expectation that they can ever improve. Others defend themselves against the need to understand topics by asserting that explanations only confuse children, and since they, the students, have learnt to 'do' the topic without any particular understanding there is no need to trouble themselves further. The lecturer will often have to work quite hard at getting the students to think about and discuss the mathematical activities that they are carrying out. Mathematically weaker students often just carry out the instructions given with little appraisal of the mathematical meaning of the activity and find it extremely difficult to pose themselves mathematical questions about what they are doing. One effect of this is that they can react badly to being set activities which they regard as childish, even if carrying them out, thinking about them and discussing them were in all other respects an excellent route to understanding the topic in question. That is to say they see only the surface activity, which may look like a child's activity, and fail to construct opportunities for thier own mathematical growth.

4. Effort vs. reward

We have conducted two studies to evaluate computer-based methods for student teachers. In both studies students used the programming lnaguage LOGO and made substantial use of its graphics facilities (McArthur [5]). All the students in both studies were taking a three year primary school teaching diploma. In the first study, 15 volunteers were recruited in a local College of Education from students with self-confessed difficulties with mathematics. These students learned the programming language, were given Rees' (1974) test and were observed and recorded on teaching practice. The observation and subsequent discussion, together with the test results, was used to determine which mathematical topics they should explore through writing programs. The work of three students was observed in detail, in particular how they learned LOGO and the way that their understanding of mathematics was affected by the programs that they wrote.

Our philosophy at the start was influenced by Papert [6], [7], one of the originators of LOGO. We wanted the students to become competent enough LOGO programmers to explore mathematical processes and we believed that problem-solving aspects of this activity were themselves valuable.

Many of the students worried about the initial period spent learning LOGO, both because of the time it took from their crowded timetable and because they could not see the immediate relevance to their future careers. Those who persevered and started to use LOGO to explore areas of mathematics in which they had difficulty were immensely pleased with the personal mathematical discoveries that they made, even if they remained pessimistic about their ability to understand the rest of mathematics. One student's comment about the effect of her LOGO activity was that she was "slightly more confident, but don't think that anything could make me feel completely confident".

As is often reported in computer-based educational innovations, the students were obviously highly involved in the work, although the fact that the students were volunteers was a factor in their attitude. But it was clear that some of them were initially sceptical about the eventual value of learning programming and hence about spending time on it even though they enjoyed it. The difficulty was compounded by the rather narrow view taken by some of the students about mathematics and about their professional responsibilities, i.e. the strategy of avoiding explanations alluded to earlier. The lesson for us was that the mathematical relevance to the student's future career had to be stressed from the start. The obvious links between the graphics features of LOGO and mathematics, e.g. angles and distance, were much more important in this respect than vaguer references to problem-solving used as a means of motivating the learning of other parts of LOGO.

In the second study, the students were not expected to spend time becoming competent LOGO programmers before starting on the mathematics work proper. They were introduced to LOGO features as and when necessary as part of the mathematics course they took. Now the focus of their activity was shifted from planning and writing LOGO programs to running pre-defined procedures and discussing the mathematics of their observed behaviour.

This second study used 'conscripts' from a different College of Education. The mathematics staff selected 12 second year students and 9 third year students who needed extra mathematical help. The students undertook a computer-based course of work on Shape and Number. They were given various pre- and post-tests of both attitude to mathematics and performance in mathematics. The 12 second year students were divided randomly into an experimental and control group of 6 students each. The 6 students in the control group followed the College's standard course in Shape and Number while the experimental group undertook the computer based work at the University.

What follows is only a brief outline of the results; more details are given in du Boulay and Howe [3]. Both the second and the third year students had enjoyed mathematics at school much less than their peers who had not been selected for extra mathematical help. There was imbalance between the second year experimental and control groups. The former liked teaching more and disliked maths more than the control group at the start. By the end of the year, the students in the experimental group had grown in their dislike of mathematics and maintained their attitude to teaching mathematics. The third year group improved in attitude to maths and to teaching mathematics.

Scores in a general maths pre- and post-test showed small and mostly non-significant improvements in all groups. In tests geared more specifically to the content of the course, the second year experimental group improved more than the control group, though even at the end of the study their results were not very good. The third year group improved in the test on Shape but not in that for Number, but again even after their improvement their final Shape scores were still not good. In general the small numbers in the groups and the high variance within the groups made comparisons difficult.

Compared to the volunteers worked with in the first study, the students who took part in the second one were conscripted. Also, they were given much less opportunity to write their own programs and get immersed in the consequent complexities. As a result these students showed much less involvement with the work and made fewer of the obvious personal mathematical discoveries that had been so delightful to observe in the first study. However they did not have to expend a large amount of preliminary time and effort mastering LOGO (though they did have to cope with a rather slower system) and spent most of their time thinking about mathematics rather than programming. This tradeoff between the effort and time expended on learning programming and the rewards in terms of personal satisfaction and insight is difficult to resolve for student teachers who have a crowded timetable and who are having a lot of difficulty with mathematics.

5. Level of representation

A recurrent difficulty, related to that just discussed, was that of maintaining the work of the students at the appropriate level of representation, appropriate in the sense that it was mathematically meaningful to the students. Initially we wanted students to write all the programs that they used so that they would have an intimate understanding of how they worked and in consequence (we hoped) an intimate understanding of the mathematics that was embodied in those programs. Our view had to be modified for two reasons, one to do with programs concerned with symbol manipulation, the other to do with programs concerned with graphic output.

Take, as example, symbol manipulation program operating on fractions, a common area of difficulty among the students. The bulk of the student's attention was focused on the issue of manipulating symbols appropriately. In a program to add two fractions, having decided how to represent fractional entities, the student had to consider how the program was to deal with the two numerators and the two denominators; in a program to reduce a fraction to its lowest terms, the student had to decide how to have the program do the cancelling. While this was a valuable, though difficult, activity and helped the student think about the algorithms she used, it missed a vital aspect of the students' mathematical misunderstanding which was concerned with the broader meaning and justification of the algorithm. The dangers were that the student could be overwhelmed by programming difficulties or be sufficiently satisfied with a program that enshrined a correct fraction manipulation algorithm that she would not go on to tackle the question of why the algorithm is just so. Our observation of students indicated that it was the 'why' of algorithms rather than the 'what' that was the central difficulty. So merely rephrasing the algorithm in a computer program was not always a helpful activity.

The second reason why we modified our approach for the second study concerned programs to produce graphic output. For example, students were asked to build a program to display pictures of fractions (say as pie charts) or of fraction operations. This could easily involve the student in issues that had nothing to do with fractions but were concerned with the details of putting drawings onto the display screen. For example, in drawing a pie chart (see fig. 1) there is the question of how to draw curved lines and how to arrange that the radii are at right angles to the circumference. While this graphics work was valuable, in that it enabled some students to discover that the angle between the radius and the circumference is a right angle, it was not directly related to the problem in hand. Consequently it deflected attention away from fractions and muddled the issue.

Our response to these difficulties was to reduce substantially the amount of programming that the students undertook in the second study in favour of providing them with many pre-written programs to run. These programs were designed to exhibit a mathematical bahaviour, such as illustrating the multiplication of fractions, or carrying out some kind of computation that could be observed and investigated by the students. For example, figures 2 and 3 show the diagrams produced by two programs that were written for the students and they simply had to supply appropriate parameters and understand the diagrams. In the first, figure 2, the student enters two fractions and as a result a diagram is displayed showing a rectangle divided up into columns using the first fraction and then into rows using the second fraction. That part of the rectangle corresponding to the multiplication of the two fractions is outlined by the machine.

In the second program, figure 3, the student also enters two

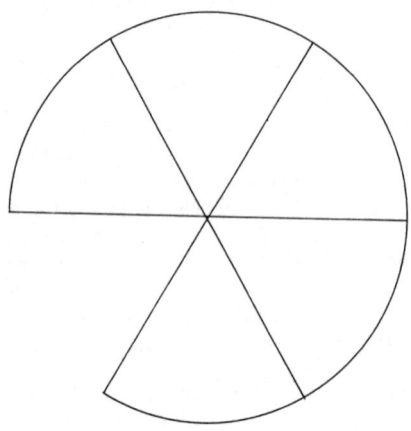

Figure 1: pie diagram representing 5/6

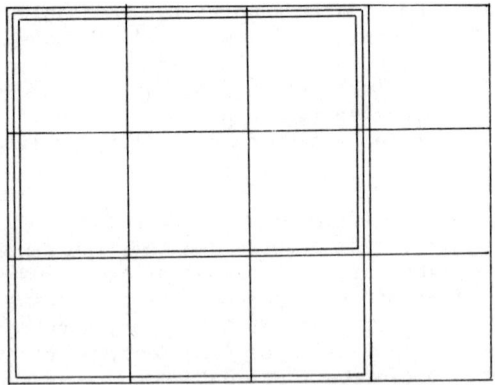

Figure 2: illustrating 3/4 x 2/3 = 1/2 by
superimposed subdivision

fractions. The program first draws a pencil shape of fixed
height and then draws a second pencil shape whose height is
transformed (by comparison with the first) in the ratio

specified as the student's first fraction). The second
fraction is used to transform the second pencil to produce a
third pencil, treating the fraction as a ratio. By comparing
the first and third pencils, a view of the multiplication of
the two fractions can be obtained. The student can enter any
number of further fractions (until the screen is full).
Each succeeding fraction is used to produce a new pencil
whose height is determined by both the fraction given and

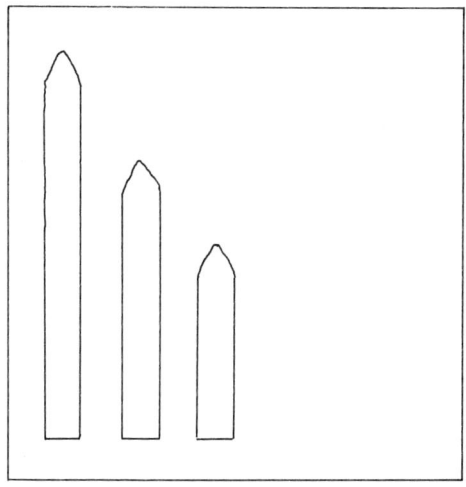

Figure 3: illustrating 3/4 x 2/3 = 1/2 by successive
vertical rescaling

the height of the previous pencil.

The mathematical topics covered were largely derived from
the work in the first study and consisted of investigations
of simple number and shape properties, but the way the
students worked was different. Only in the case of the
simplest shape tasks were the students asked to define their
own programs.

This shift of emphasis was not without its own drawbacks.
Students did not achieve that sense of program ownership and
understanding that comes from having sweated at and defined
the program, nor were we able to use programming ideas so
easily as analogies for mathematical ideas. For example, in
the first study it was possible to explain mappings in terms
of the LOGO function construct. This explanation was
suitable and successful because the student had learned how
to build LOGO functions for herself and therefore could
appreciate the analogy. In the second study, although the

students used functions, they were not required to build functions so their understanding was less.

6. Conclusion

We have described some of the problems associated with the use of computer-based methods to improve both the mathematical competence and attitudes to mathematics of students in Colleges of Education. Time constraints within a College course make choices about how to conduct this kind of work extremely difficult. We have tried two approaches in which the amount of programming to be learnt and to be carried out by the students was varied. Each approach had its advantages and disadvantages. A greater programming content meant more time was needed; there were more queries about relevance and students could get embroiled in the minutiae of programming, distracting them from mathematical issues. On the ohter hand, more programming led to greater personal involvement, a more satisfying sense of having solved a problem for oneself and more chance of making mathematical discoveries of personal value. Less programming meant that there was more time to focus on appropriate mathematical issues, the work could more easily be incorporated into the College timetable and there was no need for a programming apprenticeship. But students lost some opportunity for problem solving and did not have the benefit of having to submit their understanding (in the form of a computer program) to the scrutiny of a computer -- often a most salutory and rewarding experience.

Acknowledgements

We are grateful to the mathematics staff of Moray House College of Education and Craiglockhart College of Education, especially Mrs. Greta Clarke, for all their help in setting up and running these studies. We thank the students who took part for their patience and good humour. This work was funded by a studentship and by a research grant from the Social Science Research Council.

References

1. J.B.H.duBOULAY, Learning primary mathematics through computer programming, Ph.D. thesis, Dept. of Artificial Intelligence, University of Edinburgh, 1978.

2. J.B.H.duBOULAY, Teaching teachers mathematics through programming, Int. Journal Math. Educ. Sci. Technol., 11,

3, pp. 347-360, 1980.

3. J.B.H.duBOULAY and J.A.M.HOWE, LOGO Building Blocks:
   student teachers using computer-based mathematics
   apparatus, presented at CAL81 symposium on computer
   assisted learning, Leeds, 1981.

4. D.LUMB, Student teachers and mathematics, Mathematics
   Teaching, 68, pp. 47-50, 1974.

5. C.D.McARTHUR, LOGO user's guide and reference manual,
   Occasional paper no. 1, Dept. of Artificial Intelligence,
   University of Edinburgh, 1974.

6. S.PAPERT, Teaching children to be mathematicians vs.
   teaching children about mathematics, Int. Journal Math.
   Educ. Sci. Technol., 3, pp. 249-262, 1972.

7. S.PAPERT, Mindstorms: children, computers and powerful
   ideas, Harvester Press: Brighton, 1980.

8. R.REES, An investigation of some common mathematical
   difficulties experienced by students, Mathematics in
   School, 3, 1, pp. 25-27, 1974.

COMPUTER PROGRAMMING
IN THE MATHEMATICS CLASSROOM
AS AN AID TO UNDERSTANDING

Maurice Hart

Trent Polytechnic, Nottingham

1. Introduction

Many people who have worked with computers in schools intuitively feel that a programming activity by pupils helps their facility in the use of algebra and in their understanding of the way that particular mathematical processes operate. The Nottingham Programming in Mathematics Project has been set up to identify more clearly where a programming activity does help with mathematics at lower secondary school level, and to devise and test teaching materials that are directed towards achieving the resulting objectives. This work is particularly significant because it does help in the teaching of topics where there is a considerable failure of present methods.

That there is such a failure in the teaching of algebra in particular is noted in general terms in the DES publication "Aspects of Secondary Education in England" [1] which says on page 128:

"The time has come for a careful reappraisal of the aims and content of algebra courses, and of ways of teaching the subject. In any case, the teaching of traditional algebra has long presented difficulties in schools and it is a branch of mathematics which remains a mystery to many adults".

The particular algebraic concepts which the first year work of the project are designed to establish are variables, operations on variables, and functions. Research evidence on the present level of pupil understanding of the concept of a variable is available through the work of the CSMS project [2]. The analysis of the use of letters in that work has helped us to identify particular needs of pupils and parts of the test used have been used as a pre- and post-test in the preliminary trial of first year material.

An impresion of the Kuchemann results can perhaps best be conveyed by quoting four items from the test and giving the success rate for third year pupils on each :-

Item 1 Add 4 onto n+5 .... 68%

Item 2 Add 4 onto 3n 36%

Item 3 Multiply n+5 by 4 ..17%

Item 4 Cakes cost c pence each and buns cost b pence each.
If I buy 4 cakes and 3 buns, what does 4c +3b stand
for? 22%

These results certainly show a low level of ability to use
algebra. The report also indicated that fourth years tested
achieved results that were only marginally better.

One solution to the problem of dealing with these
difficulties in understanding which is half suggested in
"Aspects of Secondary Education in England" is to stop
teaching algebra altogether. If, as the research results
seem to show, roughly 80% of the school population cannot
cope with some relatively easy aspects of it this might seem
a reasonable solution, but surely in this technological age
we must attempt to make more people capable of reading and
manipulating algebra. There doesn't seem to be any
fundamental reason why as many people who can read or write
reasonably well cannot also use algebra.

2. Teaching algebraic concepts

While there is still much to learn about the way that
pupils' view mathematical concepts and how to affect this
view , two essentials that should be present in approaches
for pupils in the relevant age range are known. These are
(i) that there should be either a concrete embodiment of the
concept or at least a way of approach that makes a concrete
visualisation possible and (ii) that concepts need to be
contained in activities that make them meaningful to the
pupil. In many arithmetical topics it is possible to fulfil
these through the use of structured apparatus and problems
that relate to practical applications. For algebra, and the
concept of a variable in particular, it is much more
difficult to construct suitable teaching situations and this
is where the use of computer programming does help
considerably. In order to see the way that help can be given
it is useful to start with the definition of a variable
given in "The Psychology of Learning Mathematics" (Skemp
[3]) which is that "a variable is an unspecified member of a
given set". Skemp also says that the idea of a variable is a
key concept in algebra – although many elementary texts do
not explain it or even mention it. The reason why this
happens is fairly obvious; authors of textbooks and teachers
of mathematics are following the second principle outlined
above, they give their pupils experience of situations which

use the concept of a variable. Unfortunately the difficulties in understanding arise because these situations involve very different uses of the concept (as described by Kuchemann) which tend to obscure the fundamental concept rather than illuminate it. By contrast the use of programming as an introduction to algebra does fulfil both the essentials mentioned above i.e. it provides a concrete image within a meaningful activity. It also gives a very general view of the concept of a variable which is closely akin to Skemp's definition.

To illustrate this, in BASIC we use letters as labels for stores. For the pupils involved in the project this notion is approached by noting that a prime use of computers is storing and processing information,. So storing their heights, processing them and retrieving the results leads to the following programs and diagrams to illustrate the ideas.

```
-----------------
       Height
-----------------
Feet        Inches
-----------------
  5            3
-----------------
```

```
10        LET X = 5

20        LET Y = 3

30        LET M = 12*X+Y

40        PRINT X, Y, M
```

```
    Store:    Label X Y M
                -------
              Contents 5 3 63
```

This concrete image of X as a label of a store whose contents can vary, is very close to Skemp's definition of a variable, and the meaningful activity is programming or "telling the computer to do something". Within the project this is included in a teaching package which has many other facets and extensions. For example, there is much discussion between teacher and pupils about program results as illustrated via a TV monitor, pupils are encouraged to explore and create in their program writing, and are also asked to write about their results (e.g. see figures 1 and 2). The relationship with mathematical concepts is also extended well beyond the illustration given here.

3. Evaluation

The work is planned around the availability of a micro-computer system with a printer for "hands on" use by pupils. The materials for the project are designed so that each pupil needs about 15 minutes every 3/4 weeks. This means that one keyboard can service about 200 to 300 pupils. In the present state of hardware availability in schools it is not possible to achieve this without computer systems dedicated to the project. One school has such a system and they currently have three classes working on the project. One other school has helped with the preliminary trials and more are due to join in shortly. The major part of the preliminary trials of first year materials was carried out by taking one first year class through about two-thirds of the content during one term and testing them with the CSMS test. Some results of that testing are given here, though as only 24 pupils were involved the results are obviously not statistically significant. The overall results can be illustrated by the following table.

Increase/40	0	1	2	3	4	5	7	8	10	12	19
Numbers of pupils	2	3	1	4	2	3	3	2	1	1	1

The mean score increased from 23% to 36%.

Table 1   Frequency of increase
in total score (total score 40)

These figures do show that there was some considerable improvement in the overall performance of this group, though with a very wide variation between pupils. It has to be borne in mind however that this test was not devised for this purpose but to check on pupils' understanding of different uses of variables,.While it is not possible in this space to describe the full analysis of these uses and their their relation to the programming activity and test results, it may be of interest to note the results concerning the items described earlier.

Item	1	2	3	4
CSMS rate	68	36	17	22
Success pre-test	41	20	0	4
Success post-test	75	45	12	16

Table 2   Success rates in percentages
on the items from Kuchemann's test

USING A COMPUTER = PUPILS WORKSHEET

Name   SARA [surname]   Date   20.6.80

LIST

```
1    REM [initials] 20 JUNE 80
20   LET X=12
30   LET Y=8
40   LET M=12*X+Y
45   PRINT "YEARS","MONTHS","TOTAL MONTHS"
50   PRINT X,Y,M

>READY
RUN
YEARS          MONTHS   TOTAL MONTHS
12   8         152
```

THIS PROGRAMME WAS TO SHOW OUR AGE IN YEARS AND MONTHS AND
FOR THE COMPUTER TO WORK OUT THE TOTAL MONTHS. TO START TYPE YOUR
PROGRAMME, NAME AND THE DATE. THEN TYPE 20 LET AND PUT YOUR
AGE IN YEARS INTO A STORE BOX, LABBLED X SO IT WOULD BE X=12.
THEN LABLE ANOTHER STORE BOX Y AND STORE THE MONTHS IN THAT BOX
E.G. Y=8. THEN TYPE 40 LET AND LABLE ANOTHER BOX M AND IN THAT
STORE 12*X+Y WHICH IS 12 * YOUR AGE IN YEARS + YOUR AGE IN MONTHS
(THE COMPUTER WILL STORE YOUR TOTAL MONTHS IN THAT BOX). THEN
TYPE 50 PRINT X,Y,M. YOU MAY THEN WANT A HEADING YEARS, MONTHS
AND TOTAL MONTHS SO TYPE 45 PRINT IN INVERTED COMMAS YEARS, MONTHS
AND TOTAL MONTHS. YOU HAVE TO PRESS RETURN WHEN IT GETS TO THE
END OF THAT LINE. THEN LIST AND RUN THE PROGRAMME AND PRINT IT
ON THE PRINTER BY TYPING LIST AND RETURN AND THE RESULTS ARE ABOVE.

Figure 1. An example of a pupil's worksheet

<u>USING</u> <u>A</u> <u>COMPUTER</u> <u>–</u> <u>PUPILS</u> <u>WORKSHEET</u>

Name   ᴅᴀᴠɪᴅ [surname]   Date

Tᴏ ᴘᴜᴛ ᴜʀᴇ ꜱʜᴏᴇ ꜱɪᴢᴇ ᴀɴᴅ ʏᴏʀ ʜᴇɪɢʜᴛ ɪɴ ᴛᴏ ᴀ ᴄᴏᴍᴘᴜᴛᴇʀ ʏᴏᴜᴏ
ʜᴏᴠ ᴛᴏ ᴘᴜᴛ ᴛʜᴇ ʜᴇɪʜᴛ ᴀɴᴅ ꜱʜᴏᴇ ꜱɪᴢᴇ ɪɴ ᴛᴏ ᴀ ᴄᴀʟᴏᴍ ᴍᴀʀᴋᴛ ʙʏ ᴀ
ʟᴇᴛᴇʀ ᴀɴᴅ ɪᴛ ᴡᴇʟ ꜱᴛᴏᴛ ɪᴛ. Tʜᴇʏꜱ ᴀʀᴇ ᴛʜᴇ ᴡᴏɴꜱ ɪ ᴅɪᴅ.

```
LIST                                LIST

1    REM [initials] 19 6 80         1    REM [initials] 19 6 80
10   LET B=17                       10   LET A=5
20   LET C=9                        20   LET B=0
30   PRINT B,C                      30   PRINT AB

>READY                              >READY
RUN                                 RUN
17        9                         0

>READY                              >READY
                                    30   PRINT A,B
                                    LIST

                                    1    REM [initials] 19 6 80
                                    10   LET A=5
LIST                                20   LET B=0
                                    30   PRINT A,B
1    REM [initials] 19 6 80
10   LET A=4                        >READY
20   LET B=2                        RUN
30   PRINT A,B                      5         0

>READY                              >READY
RUN
4        2

>READY
```

Figure 2. Example of a worksheet by a 'remedial' pupil

Besides noting the very big improvement in the less
difficult items it is interesting to see that the post-test
results correspond closely with the CSMS figures for third
years. Some interviewing of pupils undertaken since these
trials has given a further indication that first year pupils
find questions like "Add 4 onto 3n" conceptually difficult,
rather than a simple lack of knowing what the notation "3n"
means.

4. Conclusion

The relationship between research activity concerning pupil
understanding and the use of programming certainly promises
to be a very fruitful one. More details of the preliminary
trials, including the teaching materials, further test
results and examples of pupils' work are given elsewhere
[4].

References

1. H.M.S.O., Aspects of Secondary Education in England, 1979

2. D.KUCHEMANN, Children's Understanding of Variables,
   Mathematics in School, 8,2, 1979

3. R.R.SKEMP, The Psychology of Learning Mathematics,
   Penguin, 1971

4. M.HART, The Nottingham Programming in Mathematics Project
   - Report no. 1, Finance Office, Trent Polytechnic,
   Nottingham, 1980

MOVING LOGO INTO
A MATHEMATICS CLASSROOM

Jim Howe and Peter Ross

Department of Artificial Intelligence
University of Edinburgh

1. Introduction

We have installed six Terak microcomputers in a mathematics
classroom in an Edinburgh Secondary School where they are
being used an an integral part of the first-year modular
mathematics course. When we began our research about 10
years ago, we used the computer as an artificial teacher:
more recently we have concentrated on the task of providing
computer-based facilities for carrying out mathematical
experiments. Instead of being used to ask questions and
check answers, the computer is programmed to simulate a
mathematical system, for example, a geometry system for
representing regular shapes, or a co-ordinate geometry
system, or a system for manipulating sets, and so on. The
pedagogical objective is to get a child to understand a
mathematical problem arising in such a system by having him
build and/or experiment with a model of the process for
solving that problem, expressed in computer program form. In
other words, our approach is to provide a child with kits of
mathematical parts, matched to his current level of
understanding. Just as a child experiments with mechanical
mechanisms by building and running physical models made out
of Mecanno construction kits, he is able to experiment with
mathematical mechanisms by building and running symbolic
models constructed from kits of mathematical parts [5].

It is illuminating to consider what is involved in using a
kit of parts creatively. Take Mecanno. It is a collection of
metal strips, plates, brackets and so on, that can be bolted
together to form working models of such things as cars,
lorries or cranes. To the uninitiated a box of Mecanno parts
is a bewildering collection of lumps of metal. Give a box
of Mecanno to a novice and he makes little sense of the
parts: the models he builds are unrealistic, and mechanisms
that function correctly are something of a rarity. The point
here is that learning to use a modelling system creatively
and succesfuly involves a long period of learning. In the
case of Mecanno, this period of apprenticeship can be
several years. Consider what a child has to learn in order
to use Mecanno well:

1) He has to become completely familiar with the range of components, e.g. strips, plates, tubes, axles, gearwheels.
2) He has to learn the basic operations for assembling components to form models, e.g. making measurements, establishing correct relationships between parts.
3) He has to learn about the structure and the mechanism used in the machine being modelled so he can represent their essential features, e.g. the structure of a mechanical grab and its winding gear.
4) To represent these structures and mechanisms successfully in Mecanno, he has to learn to apply important general knowledge about mechanical engineering concepts, e.g. the importance of triangular bracing, the use of plates to provide stiffening, the need for standardisation of parts for interchangeability, and so on.
5) He has to learn how to plan an assembly sequence, breaking an object into sub-parts, e.g. chassis, suspension, steering gear, gear box which can be built separately but are subject to mutual constraints when brought together.
6) Finally, he has to cope with any mismatches occuring between the plan and its execution in terms of the available components, making modifications to overcome problems not anticipated at the design stage.

So learning to use Mecanno creatively is a formidable undertaking, requiring a great deal of time and a great deal of help and guidance. But the manufacturers realised this situation: they organised the teaching most carefuly. First, they designed a series of Meccano models of objects such as cars, cranes, bridges, and so on, which ranged from very simple models made from a few components which were but sketchy representations of the real objects to highly elaborate models, made out of many hundreds of components, which could simulate a working system. Next, projects were graded into 10 levels of difficulty. Then, 10 standard sets of components were made up, each set containing the parts required for asembling any object encompassed by a particular level of difficulty provided the detailed assembly instructions were followed. Conversion kits, containing the components needed to increment from one level to the next were also provided. We can see that the implicit teaching strategy was to match projects to a child's level of expertise in assembly, beginning with a small set of components and a few simple tasks and gradually widening the scope to keep pace with his growing confidence and experience. This approach provides the close guidance a novice needs on being introduced to new skills, new concepts and new ideas. Yet it allows him to experiment and, if able, to be creative by introducing structural variations and implementing his own designs.

The Mecanno analogy has been pursued in detail because it illuminates two key problems which must be tackled before mathematics can be taught successfully through programming. The first is the problem of designing an appropriate language, and the second is the problem of deriving a method of teaching a child to use the language creatively. We will consider each in turn.

2. Designing an appropriate language

Using the computer as a modelling tool resembles using Mecanno because the computing activity centres on using an appropriate language to describe a mechanism for solving a maths problem. Just as the designers of Mecanno had to decide what components should be provided, and how they would be combined to form meaningful structures and mechanisms, the designer of a computer-based modelling system has to decide what primitive instructions should be included in the modelling language, and how they might be conmbined to form models. This is the first problem. A solution is to design a very high-level programming language with a powerful but limited set of primitive instructions from which a pupil, or a teacher, can assemble and name his own procedures for doing any computable task in a particular maths domain. Once built these procedures become part of the language and may be re-used in the definition of other procedures. This ability to build and name personalised procedures is the key feature of the LOGO programming language used in our research.

Let us take a simple example: the task of teaching a 12-year old child some of the properties of regular plane shapes. The first problem is that of providing a suitable kit of programming language parts for this topic. Seymour Papert's solution is called "turtle geometry" - a kit of commands for moving a mechanical drawing pen around a drawing surface, for example FORWARD <a distance>, RIGHT <an angle> [8]. Using these commands, an equilateral triangle can be constructed by entering in:

```
FORWARD 100
LEFT 120
FORWARD 100
LEFT 120
FORWARD 100
LEFT 120
```

As each command is received by the computer, it is executed and forgotten. Alternatively, the commands can be made into a named procedure:

```
BUILD 'TRIANGLE   {the procedure will be called
                                    TRIANGLE}
    FORWARD 100
    LEFT 120
    FORWARD 100
    LEFT 120
    FORWARD 100
    LEFT 120
END
```

This is stored in the computer's memory and is not executed until the user types the name "TRIANGLE". Moreover, having been given a name, the computer can find it again at some future time when it can be re-executed, thus avoiding the need to re-define a procedure each time it is required.

But notice that the triangle is made from repetitions of pairs of instructions, namely FORWARD 100 and LEFT 120. A more elegant formulation of the problem wouod be to decompose it into two parts, and make a super-procedure and a sub-procedure. The sub-procedure is constructed as follows:

```
BUILD 'SIDE
    FORWARD 100      {this procedure just draws a line
    LEFT 120          and turns at the end}
END
```

The super-procedure becomes:

```
BUILD 'TRIANGLE
    REPEAT 3 SIDE
END
```

Some further examples show how a child (or his teacher) can extend the modelling language by building up named procedures, and using them as new language primitives. For example, a procedure DIAMOND could be built from two TRIANGLE instructions and two turn instructions:

```
BUILD 'DIAMOND
    TRIANGLE
    RIGHT 60
    TRIANGLE
    LEFT 60
END
```

These new primitives, TRIANGLE and DIAMOND, are less powerful than the primitives from which they are assembled because they incorporate fixed values for side length and change of heading. But it is a simple matter to re-design them to acceptable variable values as inputs. For example:

```
BUILD 'TRIANGLE 'SIDELENGTH
    REPEAT 3 FORWARD VALUE 'SIDELENGTH AND RIGHT 120
END          {SIDELENGTH is the name of an input}
```

allows a user to adjust the size of the triangle drawn by
typing in the procedure name followed by a number. But now
he can also change the size of any diamond shape since the
DIAMOND procedure will be given a 'SIDELENGTH input and will
pass the numerical value assigned to SIDELENGTH to the
TRIANGLE sub-procedures.

But besides assisting the user to build commands
appropriate for a particular task, the task itself must be
selected so that the mathematical knowledge needed to solve
it is in line with a pupil's expertise. This is analogous to
the levels of difficulty in the Meccano system. We can see
how this is achieved in Papert's turtle geometry system:
many 10-12 year old children can manipulate the system quite
successfully since they have an intuitive understanding of
moving and turning, gained through their own body movements.

Suppose, however, the task was to construct irregular
shapes. The child would need to use a drawing system based
on co-ordinates and vectors. But since a 12-year old child
is too young to be introduced to trigonometry, rather than
expect him to build co-ordinate geometry procedures out of
primitive LOGO instructions, he should be given appropriate
procedures, such as PLOT [x,y] and JOINUP [x1,y1] [x2,y2].

Of course, the situation would be different if we were
dealing with a 16-year old pupil. Then we would be
interested in his ability to understand and build the kinds
of primitives given to the 12-year old child.

Although we have been using geometries as examples, at
Edinburgh we have successfully constructed primitives for a
range of topics in Arithmetic and Algebra, taught in first
year in secondary school (age 11-12). These are shown in
Table 1.

3. Teaching modelling skills

The problem which we identified in pursuing the Mecanno
analogy is that of teaching a child modelling skills. The
way in which the computer is used in a class reflects a
teacher's beliefs about teaching and learning. Some prefer
to use it in an open-ended fashion, identifying interesting
tasks, introducing a child to new ideas, new comcepts and
new techniques as and when the need arises. This is the
approach favoured for example by Papert at MIT [8] and Dwyer
at Pittsburgh [4]. But it is illuminating to consider what a
child has to learn in the course of using just one of the

Algebra

Sets 1 (membership, subsets)
Sets 2 (union, etc.)
Sets 3
Open sentences
Solution sets
Clock arithmetic
Graphs
Graphs of sentences
Pictures of multiplication
Areas of rectangles
Replacing variables
Commutative law

The numberline
Problems on the numberline
Solving equations 1
Solving equations 2
Solving equations 3
Formulae
Adding signed numbers
Subtracting signed numbers
Relations between sets 1
Relations between sets 2
Associative law
Distributive law

Geometry

Circles round a point
Polygons
Stars
Judging angles
Co-ordinates

Arithmetic

Fibonacci series
Factorials and powers
Multiples
Factors
Decomposing numbers
Binary addition

Table 1

many kits of parts available. Again, we take turtle geometry as our example:

1) He has to become completely familiar with the language components, e.g. FORWARD, BACKWARD, LEFT, etc.
2) He has to learn how to assemble components to form descriptions of processes, e.g. to build procedures, use inputs, etc.
3) He has to learn about the structures and mechanisms being modelled, e.g. drawings of regular plane shapes.
4) He has to understand basic mathematical concepts, e.g. straight line, arc of a circle, angle as rotation.
5) He has to learn how to plan drawings, e.g. breaking down a complex drawing into a set of more familiar sub-parts which can be constructed separately, but which are subject to mutual constraints when brought together.
6) He has to learn to cope with mismatches between the planned behaviour and the actual behaviour of the program, making modifications to get rid of bugs in the program and in his understanding of the process.

Clearly this is a formidable teaching task. Again the

Meccano analogy is helpful. Like the designers of the
Meccano system, when dealing with novices we believe that
there is a need for a structured approach, related closely
to the existing mathematics curriculum. In our work, we
have based our teaching on worksheets designed for self-
paced study. Somewhat like a Meccano manual, a typical
worksheet introduces a mathematics topic or a programming
topic, provides specimen procedures, and sets exercises
which can be solved by using these procedures. For example,
after spending time running and altering programs which
describe particular shapes, a child's attention can be drawn
to the fact that each program contains repetitions of the
pair of instructions "move forward and turn". For example:

```
DEFINE "PENTAGON          while   DEFINE "PENTAGRAM
FORWARD 100 and LEFT 72           FORWARD 150 AND LEFT 144
FORWARD 100 AND LEFT 72           FORWARD 150 AND LEFT 144
FORWARD 100 AND LEFT 72           FORWARD 150 AND LEFT 144
FORWARD 100 AND LEFT 72           FORWARD 150 AND LEFT 144
FORWARD 100 AND LEFT 72           FORWARD 150 AND LEFT 144
```

produces   produces

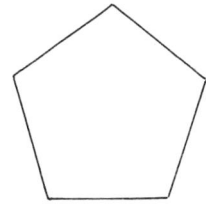

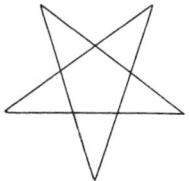

Now he can be encouraged to generalise by constructing a
program for producing a class of regular shapes when
supplied with appropriate inputs. For example:

```
BUILD 'POLYGON 'NUMBEROFSIDES 'SIDELENGTH 'ANGLE
   REPEAT VALUE 'NUMBEROFSIDES FORWARD VALUE 'SIDELENGTH
   AND LEFT VALUE 'ANGLE
END
```

By running the polygon program, varying the values of the
input parameters in a systematic way, he begins to
understand the relationships between families of quite
different shapes. In a sense, this is rather like using
Spirograph drawing wheels to construct patterns: different
combinations of wheels produce novel and unpredictable
patterns. However by using LOGO the child learns how
apparently quite different patterns relate, namely in terms

of distance and angle, and so he is able to go on to describe complex shapes in terms of the repetitions of simple drawing procedures. In other words, LOGO provides a language for describing how shapes are constructed; Spirograph does not. Even if a less able child is unable to construct the generalised procedure by himself, by acquiring a reading knowledge of the language and by experimenting with a polygon procedure supplied by the teacher as a "concept demonstration", he will acquire some insight into the underlying mathematics. In other words, even at a particular level of representation, the conceptual difficulty can be adjusted to match the ability of each individual child.

4. Preliminary evidence of benefit

The evidence yielded by an evaluation study which we ran in our laboratory suggests that this approach to mathematics can benefit the less able child. We implemented a dialect of the LOGO programming language on the University's computer and set up a programming classroom in the Department, equipped with teletypes and various drawing devices. Our pupils were 11 - 13 year old boys of average and below average ability, recruited from a neighbouring boys' school. They were divided into two groups, each containing 11 boys. The experimental group came to our programming classroom during normal school hours to work with the computer, whereas the control group followed the normal school timetable. The boys' performance on various tests were recorded at the beginning, during and at the end of the experiment which continued over two school years (P7/S1).

We approached the teaching task in two distinct phases. During a boy's first year in the project, we taught him computing concepts and techniques, our objective being to make him feel as comfortable as possible about building, or at least interpreting, programs. We believe that a novice's ability to learn programming is impeded by the fact that he lacks an adequate mental representation of the machine he is trying to use. What he needs is a description of the machine, pitched at a level of detail appropriate to the computational events for which he requires an explanation. For example, the division of the computer's Central Processing Unit into an Arithmetic Unit and a Control Unit is not described because the novice will not encounter anything in the course of working with LOGO that would indicate the existence of this division of function. We call this simplified description of the language's operation within the machine a "virtual machine". Its purpose is to provide a model as a context for introducing programming concepts, for interpreting the machine's responses and for establishing a small vocabulary for talking about programs and the activity of programming [2].

Taking such a virtual machine as context, we taught
programming by means of a self-paced series of worksheets
which introduced computational ideas such as procedures and
sub-procedures, variables and recursion; problem solving
tactics like decomposition, and the use of debugging skills
such as running a trace facility to get a commentary on the
execution of a procedure. These worksheets form an ordered
set [3].

In the second year, in practice the first year in secondary
school, the emphasis shifted to using programming to explore
school maths topics, in arithmetic, geometry and algebra,
from the Scottish maths curriculum. These are listed in
Table 1 above.

In passing, it should be noted that our pupils appear to go
through three overlapping stages in their learning and use
of LOGO. Initially, their activity seemed to be entirely
'product oriented' - in other words, their main objective
was to get pleasurable drawings irrespective of how they
were achieved, even to the extent of ransacking other
pupil's files in the search for solutions. Next, the pupils
became 'style conscious' - in other words, they tried to
construct elegant, sophisticated programs, influencing their
general conception of approved LOGO programming practice,
even when elaborate programs were not especially appropriate
to the task. The third and final stage was the emergence of
an 'analytic' style - in other words, pupils who reached
this stage used the programming resource as a scratch pad
for reducing some mathematical difficulty, and their work
could only be properly understood in the context of the
problems they were trying to solve. Further details are
given in [6].

When considering the effect on their mathematics, the
interpretation of the results is a little complicated since
the control group boys were drawn from a parallel class, and
the NFER Basic Maths Test given at the beginning of the
study showed the control group's performance to be
significantly better at the 5% significance level. In fact,
when the Basic Maths test was re-administered at the end of
the project, both groups had improved from pre- to post-test
(at 1% level) and the difference between groups was no
longer significant. In other words, the experimental group
had closed the gap.

Further evidence was available from five school mathematics
tests given to all boys in the year. The scripts for boys
taking part in the study were re-marked and ranked. This
ranking was compared with their ranking by the school at the
mid-point in the project, when transferring from junior to

senior school. The outcome was that just about half of the members of the experimental group improved their "standing", whereas only one boy in the control group improved.

An item analysis of these tests suggested that the experimental group's performance on algebra topics such as solving for x, forming and solving equations, solution sets and mappings was marginally better than that of the control group. A similar advantage was shown in the experimental group's scores in individual items on the Chelsea Algebra Test. These were the topics in algebra dealt with by the worksheets.

When consulted, the teachers were clearly of the opinion that the experimental group pupils "could argue sensibly about mathematical issues", and "could explain mathematical difficulties clearly", but rated control group boys poorly on those abilities. For additional details, see Howe et al, [7].

Although these results are encouraging, it would be easy to argue that they are not due to the computer-based approach but can, instead, be attributed to the influence of other factors not controlled in the study (though an investigation by Bjork et al., [1], using the BASIC programming language, supports its conclusions). For example, because the computer-based work supplemented classroom mathematics work, it could be argued that the improvement ought to be attributed to the extra time spent doing maths; or it ought to be attributed to the close personal attention given to each boy by the University investigators; or again it might be attributed to a "Hawthorne effect" brought about by being involved in an experiment "at the University". In answer to this last criticism, that the results reflect a Hawthorne effect, the data from attitude tests given at the beginning, mid-point and end of the study show that the boys were very enthusiastic at the beginning of the project, that they were distinctly less positive at the half-way stage, with a further shift to neutrality taking place during the second year. So we conclude that the results are not attributable to motivational effects but to some other factors.

But just about any education study carried out in the laboratory is open to these kinds of criticism. The solution was to move the work into a school setting, integrating it with on-going teaching under the class teacher's supervision and control. This is the strategy being followed in a second study - the transitional study - which is now underway.

5. Transitional study in outline

The transitional study is being carried out in a state secondary school in Edinburgh, James Gillespie's High School, in collaboration with staff in the Mathematics Department. At Gillespie's, mathematics teaching is organised on a mixed ability basis during first year (12-13 years); thereafter, pupils are organised into classes by ability in the subject. The general aim of the transitional study is to embed our approach in a classroom teaching regime, and to measure the effect on the children's mathematics. To this end, the transitional study is focussing on one year's intake (1980-81) into the first year secondary classes. This intake is divided into experimental and control groups by class, each group containing approximately 80 pupils. In the case of the experimental group, about one third of their class time is devoted to computer-based mathematics. The control group, on the other hand, is following the normal teaching scheme.

For the study, we have implemented a new dialect of the LOGO language for the Terak microcomputers. Besides making the teaching materials more versatile to cope with the wider ability range, the most significant change of teaching procedure is the dropping of the one-year programming apprenticeship. Instead, programming concepts, ideas and techniques are being taught alongside the maths as and when required. Our approach to evaluation is similar to that followed in the preliminary study. Using a pre- post- test design, we are collecting evidence about four aspects of the children's work, namely change in mathematical performance, change in mathematical competence, change in attitude to mathematics and change in ability to talk sensibly about mathematics. The test material comprises standardised (NFER) tests of mathematical attainment and mathematical understanding, and unstandardised classroom maths tests. This is supplemented by classroom observation by project staff, teachers' reports, and so on. The post tests will be administered in June 1981, and the results of the study will be available in Autumn, 1981.

As described so far, the transitional study appears little different from the preliminary study. The reason is that most of the transitional problems are concerned with the provision of computing facilities, with classroom teaching and with curriculum development. At the coal face, the division of responsibility between project staff and school maths staff is relatively straightforward. Project staff are responsible for integrating the computer-based teaching materials; school maths staff are responsible for integrating the computer-based work with the normal classroom teaching regime, for taking decisions about how much time can be given over to computer-based work on a topic, both globally and for individual children; for helping pupils with programming and other difficulties as they arise, and so on. But, of course, there is also close interaction between project and teaching staff, over such matters as design of the computer-based materials.

6. Conclusion

While we hope that the outcome of this new study will be as favourable as the last, we suspect that the real effect of the approach is cumulative and will not be fully developed until pupils have experienced it for several years; the present study, we hope, is just the first phase of a longtitudinal study which will follow the fortunes of children right through secondary school. This might also provide us with the opportunity to find out whether the improvement in mathematics through programming is due to the analysis of the problem required before a successful program can be written, or to the debugging skills learned via programming, or to the partial solutions and information gleaned by running a program and tracing through its operations, or to some other, as yet unidentified, factor.

References

1. L.-E. BJORK, An introductory computer programming course and some of its effects on the teaching of mathematics, in Proceedings of IFIP 2nd. World Conference on Computers in Education, ed. O.Lecarme and R.Lewis, Amsterdam: North Holland, 1975.

2. J.B.H.duBOULAY, T.O'SHEA and J.MONK, The Black Box inside the Glass Box: presenting computing concepts to novices, to appear in International Journal of Man-Machine Studies.

3. J.B.H.duBOULAY and T.O'SHEA, How to work the LOGO machine, Dept. of Artificial Intelligence Occasional Paper no. 4, Edinburgh University, 1976.

4. T.A.DWYER, Soloworks: Computr based Laboratories for High School Mathematics, School Science and Mathematics, Jan., pp. 93-99, 1975.

5. J.A.M.HOWE, Learning through model building, in Expert Systems in the Micro-electronic Age, ed. D.Michie, Edinburgh University Press, 1979.

6. J.A.M.HOWE, Developmental Stages in Learning to Program, in Cognition and Memory, eds. Klix and Hoffman, Berlin: Deutscher Verlag, 1980.

7. J.A.M.HOWE, Teaching mathematics through LOGO programming: an evaluation study, in Computer-assisted Learning: Scope Progress and Limits, eds. Tagg and Lewis, Amsterdam: North Holland, 1980.

8. S.PAPERT, Mindstorms: children computers and powerful ideas, Harvester Press: Brighton, 1980.

LEARNER INITIATIVES IN COMPUTER ASSISTED LEARNING

J.R.Hartley

Computer Based Learning Unit
University of Leeds
Leeds LS2 9JT

1. Introduction

Computer Assisted Learning (CAL) requires the design of
languages, command sets and response conventions which will
prescribe the types of statements the user can make at the
terminal. At present, students working within author
language programs have to use small-step responses which
have been anticipated by the author. Those learning from
simulation packages must operate within the limited number
of commands, parameter labels and values permitted by the
program. Students using educational programming languages
such as LOGO are required to work within its command
structure and syntax conventions. As a consequence, within
CAL there are limitations in student-machine dialogue which
have to be accepted. Such 'conversation' is impoverished
compared with human educational discussion and is likely to
remain so in the foreseeable future. However, even within
these limitations, it is argued that the learner can be
given greater control and a larger range of initiatives than
is usual in much of current CAL work. The following sections
examine what is involved in learner control, consider
arguments for and against giving initiative to the learner,
outline the charactersitics of mixed initiative programs
which are being developed and used at Leeds, and report
briefly on the small number of evaluative studies which have
been undertaken in this area.

2. The ingredients of learner control

Protagonists of learner control strongly argue that in much
of conventional teaching and CAL, major choices of
objectives, sequence of teaching content, and type of
material used for exposition, illustration and practice are
determined by teachers or by teaching programs to accord
with their preferences and with their decision rules. These
judgements may be wise, but they do not exercise the
student. Indeed, it has been argued [8] that they make him
system dependent in his learning. Only by allowing the
student himself to make choices, to justify them and see
their effects, will he learn about the process of making

educational decisions; only in this way will he become
self-evaluative and learn how to learn. Thus the goal of
fashioning adaptive but dictatorial programs is misplaced;
so is the argument that since students might make unwise
decisions they should be excluded from the decision-making
process.

The quest for greater learner participation is often taken
as an educational goal to which everyone should subscribe.
However, demonstrations of effective techniques of learner
control and evaluative studies of their outcomes are
relatively hard to find. The largest computer based project
is that of TICCIT (Time-shared, Interactive, Computer-
Controlled, Interactive Television). Its rationale is
perceptive and well documented ([8], [9]), and features of
its implementation together with an evaluative study of its
benefits [1] will be referred to later. Other work on study
styles and preferred modes of learning is also relevant for
it shows differences between students which present
instructional schemes largely ignore. For example Pask [10],
and Pask and Scott [11] have shown that, in free learning
situations, some students (labelled 'serialists') prefer to
gather together and relate material through a series of
relatively simple conceptual linkages. Others (labelled
'holists') tend to build more complex associations and are
more wide ranging in the material they bring together within
their mental frameworks. Pask found that learning is best
improved when the teaching style (whether externally or self
imposed) is congruent with the type of cognitive processing
which the student tends to follow.

Clearly there are difficulties in allowing student control
when the learner has an inaccurate view of his own
competence and processing style. Further, the consequences
of adopting unwise learning goals or strategies are often
not immediately apparent. Such feedback is both hard to
gather and difficult to interpret. Therefore Advisory
functions have to be part of the teaching/learning program.
Merrill has incorporated such features within TICCIT; Pask
in developing his learning system, originally labelled CASTE
[12], allows learner initiatives in choosing content and
type of instructional material, but Advice is given if these
choices appear to be too complex or ambitious with respect
to previous performances.

3. Some design features

There are several requirements for the design of CAL
materials which place educational decisions under learner
control and have the additional aim of helping the student
to learn about such decision making. These requirements
include

(i) a representation or map of the semantic content of the topic areas which form the curriculum,

(ii) a classification and labelling system for types of material (e.g. rules, examples, test items, remedial items) and their qualities (e.g. hard-easy, expressed in formal, symbolic, verbal or diagrammatic terms) which are to be used in teaching the semantic content,

(iii) a command language which allows the student to set goals, to formulate learning strategies and to implement and justify these decisions,

(iv) a specification of principles for evaluating student decisions, and for representing those guidelines which will control the advice given to him.

In the TICCIT system the topic material is partitioned into rules, explanatory examples and test questions; examples of concepts are presented in matched forms with examples and non-examples being shown together on the display screen. The content can vary on a hard-easy dimension by altering the abstract-concrete terms in which the material is expressed. A command set allows the student to browse, at various levels of detail, through the topics which make up the curriculum. Thus he can decide on his learning goals and the content sequence he will follow. The learning strategy is effected by the choice of type of material (rules, examples or test items) and its difficulty. Help is also given if requested, and this causes the system to colour-cue and highlight important parts of the text. All these dozen or so commands are made available through labelled function keys which form part of the TICCIT terminal. Thus the learner can form his objectives and through the commands control the sequence, type, and pace of the instruction. To help him make these choices an elementary Advisor can comment on progress and its relation to previous decisions.

In the TICCIT system the emphasis is placed on control of presentation variables such as content type and sequence. The teaching modes which determine the cognitive processing of the student are largely confined to exposition (telling) and inquiry (asking). However Pask and Scott [12] have attempted to give more consideration to instructional or processing variables. Rather than regarding a topic area as a network of concepts represented as declarative knowledge (i.e. concept names and attribute sets), Pask denotes concepts as procedures for establishing or deriving relations. The objectives for the student are to learn to carry out such procedures or to construct them. The topic area itself is set out as a network with nodes representing the concepts and the connecting arcs showing how one concept can be constructed, elaborated or derived from the other. The learner can elect to work on a sub-topic designated by its header-node in the network, but eventually must show his understanding of each of the concepts by being able to explain their derivation,i.e. to 'teach-back' the topic.

To learn about procedures and to explain them requires the student to be able to ask about, and answer various types of questions such as HOW?, WHY?, and WHICH?. The dialogue should encompass performance (establishing procedural links between concepts),explanation (how such procedures are constructed) and learning strategy (what procedure-sets under various header-nodes are appropriate goals in learning the curriculum). Hence, in designing CAL systems to accomplish these aims with a wide degree of learner control, a command language is needed which relates to the mental activity of the learner. In an effort to delineate some of these cognitive processes and the factors which influence them, a series of experiments were carried out at Leeds [6]. In particular, they examined student comprehension of textual material when learning topics in Applied Statistics.

4. Experiments in comprehension

The material for the first experiment concerned the definitions and properties of the binomial probability distribution. The content of approximately eighty sentences was taken from lecture transcripts and standard textbooks, and arranged in eight paragraphs. The experimental variables were the presentation mode and the semantic structure of the material. Presentation of the content was given by audio tape or by visual slides proceeding at the same rate. The structure of the topic was represented as a semantic network following techniques deriving from the LNR language of Lindsay, Rumelhart and Norman [12]. Using different arrangements of the same sentences, low-structure and high-structure versions of the content were prepared from the semantic network. Indexes of structure were calculated for these versions and the validity of the estimates was checked against the ratings of four independent judges. Thus each of the four treatment groups received the content in tape or slide form, in either high or low structured versions. In fact, each presented content had two structures, the arrangement of semantic neighbours determining the high or low order referred to above, and a serial order deriving from neighbouring sentences which were adjacent in the actual presentation. Approximately one hundred students took part in the experiment; they were rated on previous mathematics experience and allocated to the independent treatment groups following a stratified random sampling procedure.

Each group experienced the same sequence of events.The material was presented, and subjects asked to write down what they could recall. Correct order was not essential; accuracy was desirable but the sense of the passage was most important. Then the material was presented again, followed by a second recall period, after which a third and final presentation/recall sequence was given.

The results showed several features of interest. Of course, for all the treatment groups there was a significant increase in the number of sentence-propositions recalled on the three occasions. On average, 20%, 35% and 45% of the seventy-eight propositions were recalled on the first, second and third occasions respectively. Sentences tended to be recalled in their entirety or not at all, the number of propositions remembered on the first occasion (analogous to students having received a lecture, for example) was small, and the increase followed an almost linear pattern which supports a total processing-time hypothesis.

Analysis of variance showed semantic structure to be a main effect, with high-structure sentences being recalled the most. Although this difference was statistically significant, it amounted to no more than an increase of 5% - 10% in the total of propositions recalled. Of more interest were differences in the sequence of recall. The low-structure groups, even on the earlier occasions, recalled sentences which tended to cluster round their semantic neighbours, i.e. the best predictor (measured by conditional probabilities) of recall was not whether its serial neighbour had been remembered but if its semantic neighbour had been recalled. Thus, the recall sequence quickly became closer to the high structured form of the text. The interpretation is that it is the stored (and recalled) semantic structure which is progressively developed rather than a continual referencing of the presented text [5]. Incidentally, these results were not influenced by mode of presentation which caused little difference in quantity, quality or sequence of remembering between the groups.

Other evidence suggested that subjects were able to register the semantic importance of types of material making up the text, for rules were three times more likely to be recalled than were examples. Frederiksen [4] has proposed that students tend to reduce the cognitive load of comprehending new material in at least two ways. First, they ignore the conditional phrases relating to propositions (i.e. they remember the gist rather than the detail): this results in overgeneralised statements being made in recall. Second, subjects attach previous knowledge to presented concepts: this results in elaborated or inferred statements appearing in recall. In the experimental study, recalled propositions were marked as being veridical, over- generalised or inferred. The number of inferred statements particularly (and those over-generalised to a lesser extent) increased on successive occasions. This evidence supports Frederiksen's view that elaboration and over-generalisation occur at the encoding stage rather than being phenomena of 'patching' during retrieval. If the latter were the case, such inaccuracies would be expected to decrease on later occasions when more material is stored in veridical form. Thus, inferred or over-generalised statements are encoded in memory in that form and often remain that way on successive occasions as students develop their knowledge structures. Comprehension is a constructive rather than a replicative process.

A second experiment examined further the importance of coding activity on comprehension and recall of concepts. The content took parts of probability related to independent and mutually exclusive events; the presentation was in the form of text (a workbook) which varied the instructions to students in order to regulate their cognitive processing. One treatment informed the subjects that the teaching material was being tested for readability and asked them to underline any word which was more than six letters or might prove difficult to spell. Thus their processing was concentrated at a word and syntactic level. Two other treatments were derived from Craik and Lockhart's views ([2], [3]), on how depth and spread on semantic encoding aid comprehension. A second group of subjects completed questions embedded in the text which required semantic paraphrasing of the material. A third group - at corresponding points in the text - were asked to provide examples of the propositions. Thus they had to interpret the meaning of the statements within their own experience.

The content was identical for all groups (apart from the processing instructions and tasks); study time was also regulated and kept constant for all groups. Over sixty polytechnic students took part in the experiment. The material was unfamiliar to them and after being graded on previous mathematical experience, the subjects were assigned to one of the three treatment groups following a stratified random sampling procedure. When the workbook had been completed, three post-tests were given - a free-recall, a cued-recall and a comprehension test.

The semantic processing treatments (i.e. the paraphrase and construct-an- example groups) were much the superior on all post-tests. Similar results applied to the structure of the free-recall and it was notable that whereas the semantic groups recalled sentences, the other 'syntax' group recorded words and short phrases. Of the former groups the paraphrase treatment produced greater coherence and quantity in free recall; the construct-an-example group was superior on cued recall and on the comprehension test. The interpretation of this result is that the different processing instructions engaged and developed different cognitive structures (similar to the conditions of the treatment) and this

resulted in different learning outcomes. Further, students
with higher ratings on previous mathematical experience were
superior, particularly on cued recall and comprehension;
those with less mathematical competence benefited most from
the construct-an-example treatment.

Understanding and comprehension are not only influenced by
the processing instructions and tasks which are given, but
by the type of material which is presented. For example, it
is of little value asking the student to 'image' or
'picture' if the content is presented in formal or abstract
terms. In order to use previous experience, the material
and its contexts must be given in a form (perhaps through
diagrams or analogy) which allows links to be constructed
and comparisons to be drawn. A third experiment was undertaken to study such interactions. The content, on
conditional probability and Bayes' theorem, was unfamiliar
to all the polytechnic students taking part. One treatment
developed the subject formally; terms were defined and
formulae used to show the relations between concepts.
Examples were given but in abstract terms. The material was
well structured, presented by workbook, and embedded
questions required semantic paraphrase and examples to be
worked. A second treatment covered the same content in the
same sequence with the same density of embedded questions.
However, formulae were not given explicitly and the
relations were developed with reference to diagrams and
everyday experience. Approximately sixty students were
rated on previous mathematics experience and allocated to
one of the two treatment groups following a stratified
random sampling procedure. The two treatments had equal
study time and two immediate post-tests were given - a
cued-recall test and an application (problem-solving) test.
Finally, an 'impossible' but plausible problem was set.

The results were clear-cut. On the cued-recall test some
cues were formal and others were taken from the material
which used everyday themes. All the content had been
covered by both groups, but the recall performances were
clearly in line with the type of material the students had
received, i.e. the formal group were significantly the
better when formal cues were given and vice versa. Overall,
because of the balance of cues, the composite recall scores
showed no significant differences between treatment groups;
students with higher ratings of mathematics experience
performed significantly better than the others.

On the problems test which used wordings followed in
textbooks and examinations (and favoured no one group), the
questions could be worked out following either formal or
informal methods. Formulae on probability theory and Bayes'
theorem were provided, and the questions required the
student to apply his knowledge in new contexts which went

beyond what had been given in the teaching treatments. The results favoured the formal/diagrammatic group who obtained significantly higher scores, but this difference was largely due to the performances of students low in mathematics experience who obtained very much greater benefits from the informal/diagrammatic approach. Incidentally, an examination of the working methods of students largely reflected the approach of the treatment group attended. However, no candidate was successful or able to make appropriate comment on the 'impossible' problem (in which the probabilities summed to a total greater than 1.0). Thus the experiment supports previous work by Mayer and Greeno [7] and suggests that different representational forms of material interact with processing activities to develop differing cognitive structures. These can relate critically to students' previous experience and hence produce different learning outcomes.

In summary, the design of CAL materials to aid the acquisition and comprehension of mathematical concepts should give attention to (i) the semantic and serial structuring of material, (ii) the type of coding activity which is required of the learner and (iii) the representational mode in which the concepts are developed and the ways these can be related to previous experience. The sequence of learning tasks is also important to aid transfer and allow experience to be built up in a systematic way. The large individual differences shown in these experiments and the importance of the perceptions and knowledge which each individual student brings to the task (and which is often unknown to the teacher) argue for increased learner control provided that supporting advice can be obtained.

5. Learner controlled instruction

Over the past few years we have been designing and implementing CAL programs which can operate under varying degrees of learner-program control. The main application areas have been set in the teaching of Applied Statistics, and the use of mathematical methods in the Biological Sciences. Typically, students in these areas have varied mathematical experience, and in the latter application are expected to develop their mathematical skills outside their main teaching courses. A variety of CAL materials have been developed to be used in conjunction with lectures and other source materials. The main components, set for the Statistics applications, are shown in figure 1. They comprise,(i) a large number of small test-teach modules each with its own particular objective, and supported by resource materials (Student Guides), (ii) a simulation laboratory called STATS, (iii) a self-testing example bank, (iv) an

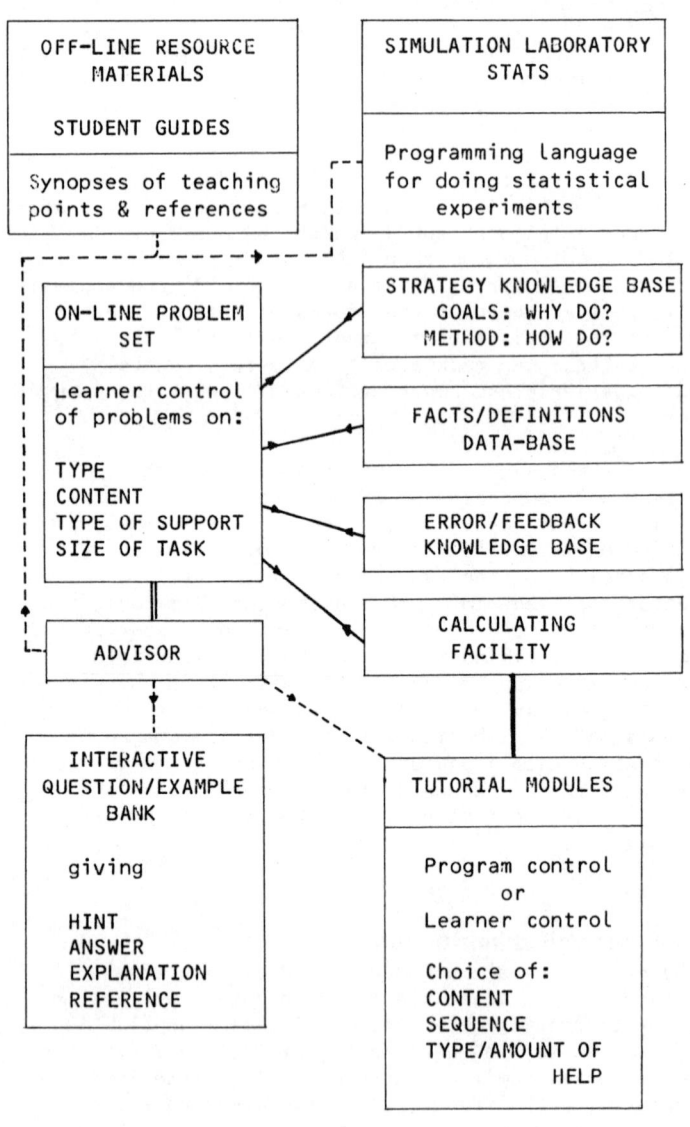

Figure 1. Types of CAL material in the Teaching System

interactive calculation and data-processing facility, and
(v) co-ordinating problem-solving modules.

The test-teach materials can be freely accessed by the
student, or guidance can be given through a control program
written by the teacher. This can select and sequence the
modules, introduce and interrelate them with comment and
supplementary teaching, and apply decision rules based on
performance, student preference or a mixture of both. Over
two hundred modules, each briefly described by a content
synopsis and arranged under topic headings, are used in
covering a typical course in Applied Statistics. The Student
Guides, which relate to the modules, summarise teaching
points, provide illustrative examples of each, together with
test questions and references for further reading.

A simulation language, STATS, provides the learner with a
statistical laboratory. The elements are data sets, and the
user can type instructions to control their generation,
editing and display, and to have arithmetical and
statistical operations carried out on them. Elementary
programs can be developed so that population probability
distributions can be specified, samples drawn, outputs
displayed in numerical or graphical form, arithmetical and
statistical operations carried out, and editing functions
used to curtail, change, or merge data-lists. These
procedures can be called successively and their outputs
compared. An advantage of using a learning laboratory for
the illustration and understanding of statistical concepts
is the activity it requires of the learner. He must
instruct the program, and the feedback (apart from a syntax
check or his instructions) is the output produced by his
program. So the student must formulate and sequence his
commands and test the output against his intentions.

By using the various types of materials, the student can,
for example, select and work through test questions in a
topic area, and from his performances decide which teaching
modules he wishes to access and study. He can illustrate
particular concepts or applications by using STATS with
associated Worksheets, and coordination can be provided
through the learner controlled problem-solving tasks. The
aim of these further programs is not only to help students
solve problems, but to help them learn in more general terms
about this process.

The student is able to choose a problem under topic headings
and, as well as typing responses in answer to questions, he
can use a command language to regulate the size of task and
the type and amount of support he needs to obtain a
solution. (A list of available commands is set out in Figure
2).

```
Whenever <> is printed the following commands
are valid:

1] To regulate size of step in working out the problem
    ANSWER← returns to wanting an answer to the problem
    STAGES← allows the question to be answered in stages
    STEPS←  takes you through the question step-by-step

2] For help on goals and strategy
    HOW DO←    gives advice on how to accomplish the
               last mentioned task
    WHY DO←    gives a reason for trying the current task
    HOW LAST←  returns to previous task and gives advice
    WHY LAST←  returns to previous task and gives reason

3] For summarising and regulating the route through
   the problem
    QUESTION← prints text of the current question
                 you selected
    REQUIRED← prints text of the question/stage/step to
                 which an answer is currently required
    BACK←       returns to the previous statement
    START QUESTION← starts the question afresh
    START STAGE←    starts the stage afresh
    START STEP←     starts the step afresh
    REMIND←     prints summary of how you got to this point
    REVIEW←     prints summary only of questions you
                 recieved and answers you have given
    STOP←       returns to **!

4] Obtaining information and feedback

    After an error of a particular type
    WHY WRONG← will give further information
    TELL←       tells the answer to the question
    <word or phrase>#← gives a definition of the word or
                        phrase (if available)
    <word or phrase>?← gives information (if available)
    CALCULATE← gives access to calculation facility
                    (FINISHED← to return)

    When
    <*> is printed, either
    SHOW←       can be typed to obtain a summary of the
                method of the last stage or the whole
                question, whichever is appropriate
    Or
    ← can be typed to move on to the next stage
       or question
```

Figure 2. Student commands for controlling teaching

The user can elect to answer the question as a whole (ANSWER mode) or in STAGES or in STEPS (where a stage is made up of several steps). Other commands allow him to access various information systems. For example, he can ask about goals (WHY DO?), in which case the program will indicate how that goal, if obtained, moves towards a solution. By asking this question successively, more stages in the solution are revealed. If the command HOW DO? is typed, the program will indicate in general terms the method by which that goal might be reached. It states how general characteristics of the task suggest that type of solution. Typing the command successively reveals more detail but if the student requires more specific help he must reduce the size of the task, perhaps by moving from STAGES or STEPS.

Other information systems relate to facts and definitions of terms and procedures which are encountered in the problems, and to the types of errors which a student makes. The program locates mistakes but does not provide the right answer unless instructed to do so by the command TELL. The learner is more likely to prefer a further attempt or to obtain information by typing WHY WRONG? The program then matches the student's answer against particular types of error, e.g. a mathematical (careless) error, an omission, an error arising from misunderstanding the context, a logical error, an answer which misses the point, or a partially correct answer. These classes of error are given consistent types of feedback for all problems in the bank. This consistency in dealing with commands helps the student to learn to use the language more easily and provides a stable framework on which to build his experience. As the programs are designed for visual display screens, further commands are needed to summarise and recall progress.

These facilities can be applied in a wide range of teaching subjects. The materials are most advanced in mathematical methods employed by the Biological Sciences and includes logarithmic and exponential functions, and the elements of calculus. Since the structure and style of the modules are standardised, computer programs have been written to translate the prestored material prepared by teachers into the runtime programs used by the students. In this way a bank of problems and associated teaching can be prepared efficiently and economically. Although developed on a larger machine, the system is being adapted for use with microcomputers.

Each student enters the system with an identifying code and an Advisor program stores all the responses he makes. The aim is to give guidance at two levels. First, on the choice of teaching obtained from the tutorial modules, the simulation exercises and the problem bank. Second, to indicate the type of problem the student should undertake and the level of support (if any) which he might seek. The aim is to enable him to work through any problem within the topic area at the answer level without calling on help from the program. Currently, detailed interviews with students as they work through materials are being used to validate and extend this guidance.

6. Some evaluation studies

Some initial evaluation studies have been undertaken at Leeds in order to enquire how students used the system and to study its effects. For example, the materials were used for teaching some sixty Psychology students the elements of experimental design. The undergraduates were randomly assigned to two teaching groups. One followed a program controlled route through the material which was regulated by individual performance levels. The other assembled facts, definitions, examples and test questions in labelled files which the student could access as he wished. Post-test results clearly favoured the program-directed group, though these benefits were largely gained by the students with less mathematics experience. However, questionnaires showed that the undergraduates gave higher ratings of satisfaction and stimulation to the learner controlled materials. A similar experiment carried out with Chemistry students (on the planning of laboratory experiments) produced equivalent results. It was clear that many students did not choose their route through the material wisely, they tended to overestimate their abilities and present their answers to test questions before they had worked through sufficient preparatory material. Even when an error had been made, they sometimes did not pick up the appropriate teaching. As a consequence, off-line pencil and paper post-tests gave inferior results to the learner control group. However, when a second extended experiment was undertaken covering a series of three related topics, the final post-tests showed that the learner controlled group eventually produced equivalent results in a shorter study time and consistently gave higher ratings for interest and congeniality.

The liking of students for learner control was also shown when thirty-six Biological Science undergraduates worked through a series of eight problems, using the command language described earlier. Half the students talked into a microphone as they worked through the modules, in order to justify and explain their decisions and comment on the difficulties they were experiencing. These protocols were tape recorded. All students completed a Mathematics pre-test and a post-test questionnaire; all on-line responses made by each student were stored. The results, which have not been fully analysed, showed that the learner control systems obtained high ratings for congeniality, effectiveness and ease of use. The mean scores on a ten-point rating line were 6.7, 7.3, and 8.1 respectively. The on-line performances also improved over the sequence of working sessions, and in general the decisions showed that students were able to upgrade the size of task and decrease the program support in a sensible manner.

The studies carried out by Pask have been referred to earlier ([10], [11]), but the largest independent study of a learner controlled system was the evaluation of TICCIT undertaken in 1975-76 [1]. Five thousand students were involved, covering two hundred sections of target courses in American community colleges. All students must have completed at least one term's exposure to TICCIT material before they could be included in the experiment. The programs served as a direct replacement of teachers so the study compared TICCIT classes with equivalent groups of students following the conventional lecture-discussion methods in the same Mathematics courses in the same college.

The results were interesting and perhaps unexpected. In the conventional Mathematics teaching, a completion rate of 50% was recorded, i.e. half the students satisfactorily received a credit grading at the end of the course. For the TICCIT group this completion dropped to 16%. Attitude questionnaires completed by these students also showed less favourable attitudes to Mathematics than did those following the lecture-discussion treatments. (Perhaps it should be noted that the criteria for course completion differed between the treatments. The TICCIT system barred progress at the end of certain sections unless satisfactory performances were recorded. The conventional treatment offered no such hurdles). However, it appears that TICCIT was producing a detrimental degree of learner control. "Programs that allow each student to proceed at his or her own pace risk losing students unable to manage their own learning." An analysis of post-test data was undertaken to compare levels of achievement. On tests closely following the material of the course, the TICCIT groups obtained scores which were, on average, more than 10% better than those who had been conventionally taught. Other post-tests based on application and problem-solving tasks showed even greater differences in favour of the TICCIT system.

In summary, there are several good reasons why learner control should be further developed. First, it seeks to enlarge the range of activities which engage the learner. He has to consider not only performance but more general goals, learning strategies and methods; he must become self-evaluative and appraise his performance in terms which will be useful on later occasions. This should have effects extending outside Computer Assisted Learning. Second, learner control, perhaps more than other forms of CAL, provides a stimulus for program designers and researchers since it raises questions of the representation of subject matter content and of learning strategies. Finally, it requires both learner and teacher/author to examine the instructional process. They must consider how it is given form and life through the dialogue and through the initiatives which participants take and share.

Acknowledgement

The author wishes to acknowledge the work of members of the Computer Based Learning Unit at Leeds University: Kenneth Tait implemented the Learner Control System and was responsible for many of its design features and applications.

References

1. D.L.ALDERMAN, Evaluation of the TICCIT Computer-Assisted Instructional System in the Community College: FINAL REPORT. Educational Testing Service, Princeton, New Jersey 08541, USA, 1978.
2. F.I.M.CRAIK and R.S.LOCKHART, Levels of processing: A framework for memory research, Journal of Verbal Learning and Verbal Behaviour,11,pp 671-684, 1972.
3. M.W.EYSENK, Levels of processing: A critique, British Journal of Psychology, 69, pp 157-169, 1978.
4. C.H.FREDERIKSEN, Acquisition of semantic information from discourse: Effect of repeated exposures, Journal of Verbal Learning and Verbal Behaviour, 14, pp 158-169, 1975.
5. D.R.GENTNER, The structure and recall of narrative prose, Journal of Verbal Learning and Verbal Behaviour, 15, pp 411-418, 1978.
6. D.HOBBS, Evaluation studies in Computer Based Learning, Unpublished Ph.D. Thesis, Leeds Polytechnic, Leeds LS1 3HE, England, 1981.
7. R.E.MAYER and J.G.GREENO, Structural differences between learning outcomes produced by different instructional methods, Journal of Educational Psychology, 63, pp 165-173, 1973.
8. D.M.MERRILL, Learner control in Computer Based Learning, Computers and Education, 4, 2, pp 77-96, 1980.

9. D.M.MERRILL and N.D.WOOD, Instructional strategies: A preliminary taxonomy, ERIC Information Center, Columbus, Ohio 43210, USA, 1974.

10. G.PASK and B.C.E.SCOTT, Strategy, competence and conversation as determinants of learning, Journal of Programmed Learning and Educational Technology, pp 240-253, 1968.

11. G.PASK and B.C.E.SCOTT, Learning strategies and individual competence, International Journal of Man-Machine Studies, 4, pp 217-253, 1972.

12. G.PASK and B.C.E.SCOTT, CASTE: A system for exhibiting learning strategies and regulating uncertainties, International Journal of Man-Machine Studies, 5, pp 17-52, 1973.

13. D.E.RUMELHART, Notes on a schema for stories, in BOBROW,D.G. and COLLINS,A.M. (eds) Representation and Understanding. Academic Press, New York, USA, 1978.

ENTAILMENT MESHES
AS REPRESENTATIONS OF KNOWLEDGE
AND LEARNING

Gordon Pask

Architectural Association, School of Architecture,
36 Bedford Square, London; Brunel University;
System Research Developments Ltd., London;
NIAS, Netherlands

and

Paul Pangaro

System Research Developments Ltd.,London

1. Introduction

Entailment meshes are a means of representing relations
between knowable topics, named, P,Q,R,S,T... in a subject
matter. Meshes consist of nodes representing topics and
boundaries surrounding those topics which (according to a
thesis or exposition made by one or several authors) are
coherent (that is, make sense together). Some basic
constructions are shown in figures 1 to 4 - though they can
be arbitrarily complex. It is important to note that the
envelopes surrounding the clusters or blocks of nodes are
patterns of coherence (not, for example, set-theoretic or
Venn diagrams); further, that there are two essential types
of overlap; collective, as shown in figures 1 and 2 (which
might contain any number of nodes) and distributive, as
shown in figure 3. Both types of overlap appear in figure
4. But certain diagrams like figure 5 are prohibited insofar
as there is not sufficient distinction to support or to
maintain the asserted coherence of the structure.

Thus, figure 1 may be interpreted as saying that topic T is
derivable from topics P and Q; P from T and Q; Q from T and
P; figure 2 that T is derivable from topics R and S; R from
T and S and S from T and R; figure 3 that topic T is
derivable from P and Q or from R and S or both, as well as
the statements interpreting figures 1 and 2, i.e. there is
more than one supportable derivation of T. In all these
cases, T,P,Q,R,S remain distinct. (T $\neq$ P $\neq$ Q $\neq$ R $\neq$ S).
However, in figure 5 there is not enough specificity to
support the asserted coherence. To see this, notice that P $\neq$
Q, but that there is not sufficient distinction to support
that contention. True, T is derivable both from M and P or M
and Q or both and that M is derivable from T and P or T and
Q, or both, but there is a derivation "P from M and T"
together with the derivation "Q from M and T" which renders
P equivalent to Q, and, as a result, contravenes (within the

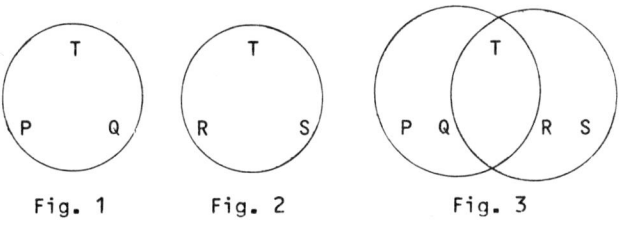

Fig. 1   Fig. 2   Fig. 3

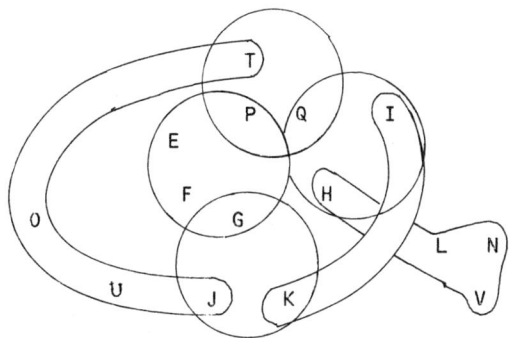

Fig. 4   Permissible but quite complex form

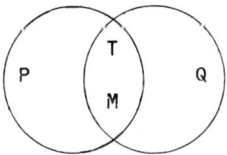   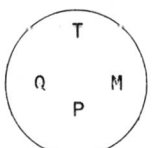

Fig.5a Prohibited form as result   Fig. 5b
     of Rule of Genoa; c.f
     figures 6-11.

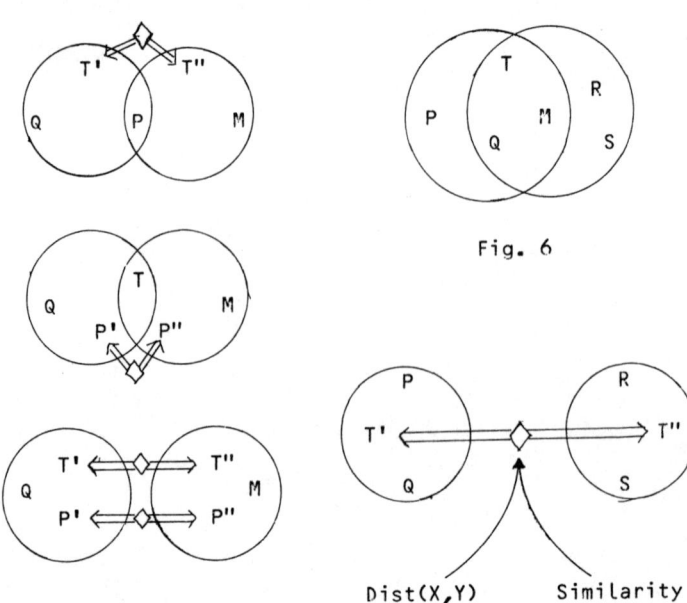

Fig. 6

Fig. 7

Dist(X,Y)   Similarity

Fig. 8

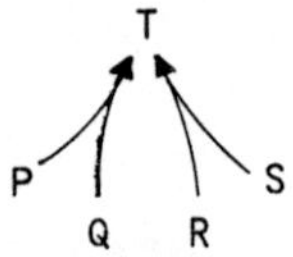

Fig. 9

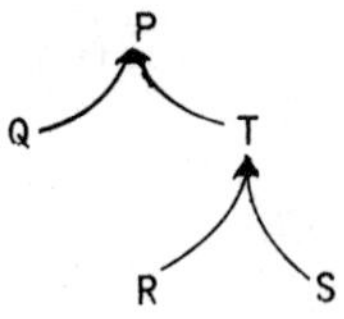

Fig. 10

Fig. 11

limits of this notations) the asserted distinction of P and Q.

One remedy, if the structure shown in figure 5a is asserted, consists in saying that really (figure 5b) the construction is collective; another lies in adding further topics (figure 6) and maintaining the now more specific distributive form. Finally, there is a series of resolutions (figure 7) in which $T \neq T' \neq T''$; $M \neq M' \neq M''$ but that although T' and T'' are distinct (lacking further information, merely independent), and although M' and M'' are distinct (lacking further information, merely independent) these pairs of terms T',T'' amd M',M'' are in correspondence (at this stage, and without further information, in one-to-one correspondence). This is expressed by the diamond notation. Of these resolutions, figure 5 amounts to relinquishing an asserted degree of coherence (namely, the distributive form); figure 6 to adding further specifity (Topic U or Topics U and V). The resolutions of figure 7 maintain the distributivity and preserve the required distinction; the final one being selected unless a direction is introduced, externally.

2. Some background

Entailment meshes were devised as a shorthand notation employed to represent the relations between "stable concepts" in the sense of conversation theory. Specifically, a stable concept is either a complementary pair $\langle \eta, \mu \rangle$, in the conceptual repertoire of a participant A,B,..., made up of a procedure η (program compiled and open to execution in a brain) and the iterative execution of this procedure, μ (a behaviour or an internal, intellectual behaviour: an image proper to A,B,..., of this execution). A stable concept may also exist if there is a class of concurrently executable procedures that are, or tend to, conflict-free execution by A or B provided they can be produced and reproduced, like Bartlett's "schemata", Wertheimer's "productive thought" or Kelly's "core constructs" [1-15], in A's or B's repertoire. Under this interpretation, a stable concept is subscripted by the repertoire A,B,... to which it belongs; for symbolic convenience "$\text{Con}_A T$" or "$\text{Con}_B T$" with the overall caveat that if "Ex" means "Execution of" then:

$$\text{Ex}(\text{Con}_A T) \Rightarrow T_A \text{ and } \text{Ex}(\text{Con}_B T) \Rightarrow T_B$$

Further, the conceptual repertoires contain operations C_A^+, C_B and C_A, C_B, like Con, but able to reproduce and produce further Con as complementary pairs. So, generally $\langle \eta, \mu \rangle$, stands for

$$\langle Con_A T, \ T_A \rangle \ \text{or for} \ \langle Con_B T, \ T_B \rangle$$

where it is legitimate to regard the execution of procedures in $Con_A T$ as demonstrations or explanations given by A and $Con_B T$ as those given by B; similarly, to regard T_A as A's description and T_B as B's description.

The operations C_A^+, C_B^+ act upon the concurrent procedures in $Con_A T$, given T_A (or $Con_B T$, given T_B) to produce some novel procedures coherent with or concurrently executable with $Con_A T$ or act upon other stable concepts, like $Con_A P$, $Con_A Q$ (or $Con_B P$, $Con_B Q$), to do the same thing (given T_A or T_B). The operators C_A, C_B act upon A's or B's actual or intellectual behaviours P_A, Q_A (or P_B, Q_B) to make T_A (or T_B). A reproductive and productive system of this kind is called "organisationally closed" and the classical forms of system-theoretic-stability are special cases of organisational closure [16].

Such an arrangement may or may not be informationally open; if it is informationally open, participants A and B may converse and, in so doing reach an <u>agreement</u> which is modelled by a <u>coherency</u> whereby concepts are shared. Of course, A and B do not usually have identical concepts, so that $\langle Con_A T, T_A \rangle$ is not identical to $\langle Con_B T, T_B \rangle$ but there are complementary pairs, shared by conversation in a language, L, reproducible in both A's and B's repertoire. For a population A,B,...N of L users, the shared and reproducible pairs are $\langle Con_{A,B...N} T, \ T_{A,B...N} \rangle$ which is conveniently abbreviated to "T" (one of the topics named by nodes in an entailment mesh) and the L meaning of the term, T.

3. Entailment mesh representation of stable concepts and agreement

The "make sense together" or "coherence" conditions expressed by figures 1,2 or 3, reflect the commonly reproducable and productive character of a conversation in which A, B, and others reach agreement, using a language L.

It is legitimate to give a liberal interpretation to the language as either natural language, or a medium, such as gesture or physical demonstration, in which it is possible to ask questions and interpret explanations; a medium like natural language, but not necesssarily a spoken language. Similarly A, B, ... the participants are liberally interpreted. For example, they may be people or groups of people sharing certain stable concepts, or "perspectives" or "points of view" which, although distinct, may be adopted by one person and coexist in one brain (in which case the A, B, ... conversations are usually unobservable ruminations or

thoughts, although they can be exteriorised under
appropriate circumstances, and observed).

The diamond shaped notation of figure 7 depicts, in static
form, a relation between distinct participants. For example,
T' in figure 7 might stand for $<Con_A T, T_A>$ and T'' for
$<Con_B T, T_B>$ and the diamond for a static inscription of the
process whereby A and B share concepts of T. Conversely,
the diamond shaped notation may also stand for an internal
comparing and contrasting of perspectives that coexist in
one person, perhaps belonging to different universes of
interpretation, say X and Y. So as suggested in figure 8,
the figure 7 distinction of independence may be refined to a
particular predicative distinction (X=Hydraulics
Y=Electricity, for instance). In each case, comparison and
contrast of participants, or perspectives, or universes, the
diamond notation, refined or not, is an analogy relation
existing in some analogical universe.

4. Some implications for education

There are several important educational consequences of
convesation theory and the entailment meshes used to depict
the internal coherences and analogy relations obtained by
conversation theory transactions. There is a sense in which
any participant can adopt any point of view, or perspective,
with respect to a body of knowledge. Unless that is done,
the knowable topics are not hierarchically ordered (there
are no absolute prerequisite topics, only those engineered
by idiosyncratic learning experience, indirectly, perhaps,
by cultural or institutional constraints). Once a
perspective is adopted a hierarchical ordering is imposed (
a "pruning", figures 9 and 10, or class of learning/teaching
strategies). In pursuing a particular learning/teaching
strategy the "pruning" is dissected and one constituent is
pinpointed (figure 11 shows one of them taken from figure
9).

Similarly, there are discernable learning styles, which,
although there is considerable generalisation for
individuals, really belong to perspectives (it may simply
happen that a person is inclined to adopt the same kind of
perspective; for example, over all "academic" or all
"scholastic", situations) which may or may not be conducive
to effective learning.

5. Further developments

A microprocessor version of a program THOUGHTSTICKER, due
chiefly to McKinnon Wood, now exists. It is able to derive
arbitrary prunings (figures 9 and 10) from an entailment

mesh, and to select components of them (figure 11), as well as accepting and monitoring expositions to form legal (i.e. coherent or analogical) entailment meshes. An other-than-authoring method of generating entailment meshes, from tactical performance in a tactical decision system (TDS) but generally applicable to expert demonstration of a subject matter, also exists.

Finally, it has been recognised that entailment meshes, which originated as a shorthand, do, in fact, amount to expressions in a protolanguage or protologic, Lp ([17], [18]), of process, coherence, distinction, and predication. As such, Lp is a kinetic entity (several implementaions exist but require multi-processor hardware) which for example, provokes an author into coherent exposition or a learner into exhibiting the style proper to any perspective taken up.

References

1. J.S.DANIEL, Conversations, individuals and knowables, toward a theory of learning, Engineering Education, Feb., pp. 415-420, 1975.

2. N.ENTWHISTLE, Symposium: Knowledge Structures and Styles of Learning: a Summary of Pask's recent research, Br. Journal Ed. Psychol., 48, pp. 1-10, 1978.

3. G.PASK, B.C.E.SCOTT and D.KALLIKOURDIS, Series of five papers, Int. Journal Man Machine Studies, 1973-1975.

4. G.PASK, Conversation, Cognition and Learning, Amsterdam and New York: Elsevier, 1975.

5. G.PASK, Conversation Theory: Applications in Education and Epistemology, Amsterdam and New York: Elsevier, 1976.

6. G.PASK, Conversational Techniques in the study and practice of education, Br. Journal Ed. Psychol., 46, I, pp. 12-25, 1976.

7. G.PASK, Styles and Strategies of Learning, Br. Journal Ed. Psychol., 46, II, pp. 128-148, 1976. 8. G.PASK, The Limits of Togetherness, Invited Keynote Address at IFIP World Congress in Tokyo and Melbourne, Proceedings ed. S.Lavington, Amsterdam and New York: North Holland, pp. 999-1012, 1980.

9. G.PASK, contributor and editor 3rd and 4th Richmond Conferences on Decision-making in Complex Systems, A.R.I., 1978 & 1980.

10. G.PASK, Final Scientific Report S.S.R.C., HR/2708.

11. G.PASK, Developments in Conversation Theory - part 1, Int. Journal Man Machine Studies, 13, pp. 357-411, 1980.

12. F.C.BARTLETT, Remembering, Cambridge University Press, Cambridge, 1932

13. G.A.KELLY, The Psychology of Personal Constructs, Vol 1 and 2, New York: Norton, 1955.

14. M.SHAW, On Becoming a Personal Scientist, London: Academic Press, 1980.

15. M.WERTHEIMER, Productive thinking, Social Science Paperbacks, London, 1961 16. F.VARELLA, Principles of Biological Autonomy, London: Academic Press, 1980.

17. G.PASK, An essay on the kinetics of language, behaviour and thought, Proceedings Silver Anniversary Meeting of Society for General Systems Reasearch, London, 1979.

18. G.PASK, An essay on the kinetics of language as illustrated by a protologic Lp, Proceedings Workshop on Fuzzy Formal Semiotics and Cognitive Processes at 2nd Congress of the Int. Assoc. for Semiotic Studies, Vienna, 2-6, 1979, Rep. Ars Semiotica, Amsterdam, 1980.

RECORDING CHILDREN'S MATHEMATICAL BEHAVIOUR

Tim O'Shea and Ann Floyd

Open University

1. Introduction

Research in the psychology of mathematical education has
been severely hampered by the lack of good longtitudinal
data. Recently we have developed a portable classroom
recording system, that enables us to collect data of a
quality previously unaccessible to researchers in this area.
We have also recently successfully carried out pilot
laboratory studies with computer-based diagnostic systems
which demonstrate the possibility of capturing precise
details of both paper and pencil working and of
distinguishing the different strategies used by children for
organising their own learning in mathematics. Our aim is to
extend the production rule models successfully applied in
two column subtraction to the construction of computational
models for a variety of topics in middle school and
mathematics.

2. The aims and methods of our research

The broad aim of this research is to better understand the
mathematical behaviour of children of middle school age. We
are interested in how children learn mathematics, how their
mathematical competence develops and how they organise their
learning. Our methods are those of the information
processing psychologist ([10], [8]). We collect protocols
of individual children's mathematical performance and then
produce computer models. We follow the modelling approach
pioneered by Young, [18], who demonstrated that production
rules could be used to model regularities in children's
problem-solving over time. One of the ways we test our
models is by incorporating them in computer based teaching
systems (the best example of this approach of incorporating
models in teaching systems is found in Woods and Hartley,
[17]).

The particular aim of our current three year study is to
examine the learning of arithmetic and story problem solving
methods by children of middle school age. We intend to
produce an explanation of both the error patterns that are

known to occur [1], and an account of the wide variation in the way children organise their learning ([14], [6]). The research depends on the availability of two pieces of micro-computer basd equipment, namely, a 'paper and pencil working recorder' using a Cyclops/Datapad and an automatic route recorder based on a Terak microcomputer.

3. Modelling arithmetic skills

In recent years the methods of artificial intelligence have been applied to understanding the strategies underlying children's arithmetic skills. One hypothesis that underlies this work is that many errors in arithmetic are principled in the sense that they do not result from carelessness but from the incorrect application of strategies that would be correct in another context. An area of arithmetic that has attracted attention recently is subtraction ([3], [19]). Research workers in this area typically start with a collection of scripts (e.g. see [2]), each being an individual child's attempt to solve a variety of problems. The errors in the scripts are then classified and related to the types of problem. Models for the individual problem-solving strategies are then induced and expressed in some computational representation. Young and O'Shea [19] have developed a model for subtraction with the following characteristics:

1) It models subtraction skill as a collection of independent rules. Each rule is a production rule [10] and has a condition part and an action part. The conditions match on elements of a written subtraction sum or on items in a working memory. The actions involve either changes to the written sum (such as decrementing a digit) or depositing an item (such as 'borrow') in the working memory. These rules can be "run" to generate actual behaviour for each problem. When more than one rule has its conditions matched by the contents of the working memory then 'conflict resolution' principles with a psychological justification are used. One such rule is that items deposited more recently in the working memory are 'stronger' than older items. When a rule is executed it results in either an addition to the working memory (this corresponds to saying to oneself, for example, "I think I should borrow now") or a change to the written sum.

2) They can account for the errors commonly seen in terms of the omission of necessary rules or the inappropriate inclusion of rules from other arithmetical tasks.

The performance of these models can be evaluated against the original data. In the case of Young and O'Shea's work their model accounts for two-thirds of their original error data. Comparing their model against the data of Brown and Burton [3], it accounts for their 15 most frequent errors. Brown and his collaborators have identified very many errors in subtraction and have suggested ways of deriving incorrect strategies from correct strategies by applying procedures that model incomplete learning and forgetting. Now both Young and O'Shea [19] and Brown and Vanlehn [4], can model subtraction at a finer level of detail than that given by data they currently use. For example the order in which a child writes down the digits in the answer to a sum can be predicted. We believe that if further progress is to be made in this area it is necessary to collect data that records finer detail. This will make it possible

    i) to take intermediate steps in the execution of an arithmetic task into account when constructing models, and

   ii) to use such data to provide a sharper test of our existing models of arithmetical competence.

4. Recording mathematical working

Our solution to the data recording problem has been to use the Cyclops audio visual system developed at the Open University [13]. Cyclops is designed for a variety of educaional applications including low-cost non-broadcast audio visual replay and audio visual teleconferencing. It records on and replays from conventional audio tapes. One of the data capturing devices that can be used is a Datapad. Together, they have enabled us to produce a protable robust system that can be taken into a classroom and used to record a synchronised protocol of handwriting, together with any verbal commentary the child may make.

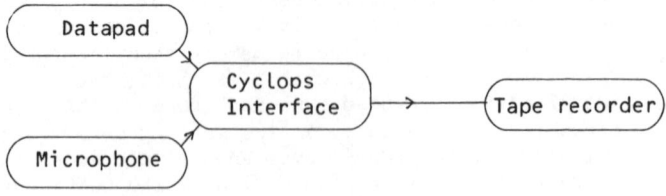

Fig.1 'Paper and pencil working' recording equipment

The Datapad and microphone can be placed on a pupil's desk. The interface box and portable taperecorder are both small and can be put in or under the desk. The pupil places her exercise book on the Datapad and works quite normally except that she uses a special pen attached to the Datapad. The

pupil is also encouraged to verbalise her mathematical
working. The recording system works well and unobtrusively.
It has been used successfully by high ability and remedial
pupils ranging in age from seven to eighteen. An example of
the data recorded is illustrated in figure 2.

{Arrows show direction of writing; words spoken by pupil}

"46 take
    away 34 is 12"

$$\begin{array}{r} 46 \\ -34 \\ \hline 12 \end{array}$$
----→

{Silence for about a minute}

"5 take away 2, no, 7 take
away 2 is 5, 1 take away
5 is 4"

$$\begin{array}{r} 52 \\ -17 \\ \hline 45 \end{array}$$
←----

"44 take
    away 24 is 20"

$$\begin{array}{r} 44 \\ -24 \\ \hline 20 \end{array}$$
----→

"50 take
    away 49 is 1"

$$\begin{array}{r} 50 \\ -49 \\ \hline 1 \end{array}$$
----→

"90 take
    away 58 is 32"

$$\begin{array}{r} 90 \\ -58 \\ \hline 32 \end{array}$$
----→

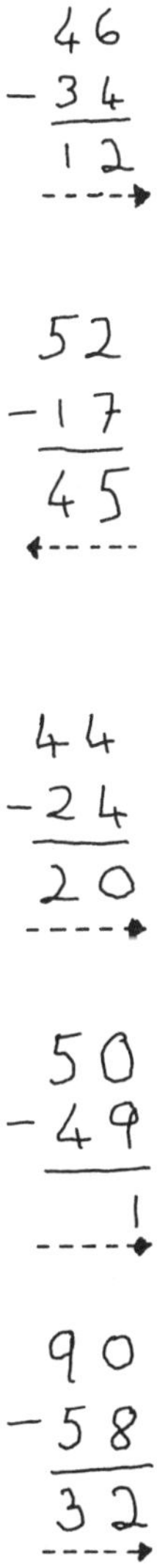

"60 take
    away 19 is 41"

$$\begin{array}{r} 60 \\ -19 \\ \hline 41 \end{array}$$
----▶

"67 take
    away 49 is 28"

$$\begin{array}{r} 67 \\ -49 \\ \hline 28 \end{array}$$
-----▶

"420 take
    away 311 is 109"

$$\begin{array}{r} 420 \\ -311 \\ \hline 109 \end{array}$$
----▶

{Silence for a short time}

"563 take
    away 274 is 309"

$$\begin{array}{r} 563 \\ -274 \\ \hline 309 \end{array}$$
----▶

"486 take
    away 226 is 263"

$$\begin{array}{r} 486 \\ -223 \\ \hline 263 \end{array}$$
----▶

"5 take away 2 is 3, 2 take
away 4 can't do, divide by
10, pay back 1, 12 take away
4 is 8, the 6 take away 3 is 3"

$$\begin{array}{r} 6\,\overset{1}{\cancel{2}}\,5 \\ -\overset{3}{\cancel{4}}\,42 \\ \hline 3\ \ 83 \end{array}$$
◀----

"721 take
    away 632 is 89"

$$\begin{array}{r} 721 \\ -632 \\ \hline 089 \end{array}$$
----▶

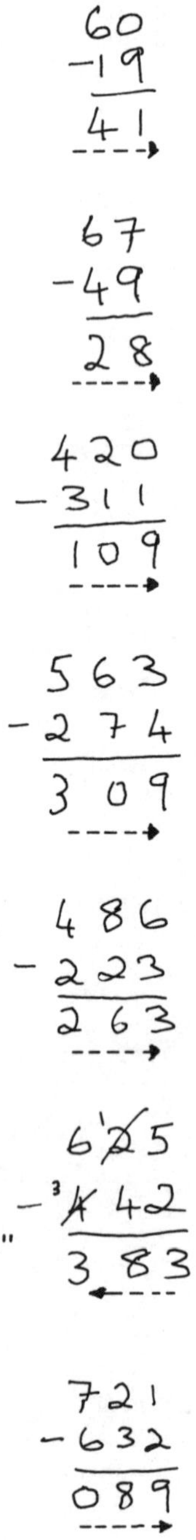

Fig. 2 A child's record taken from a CYCLOPS tape

Note that we can discriminate between left to right and right to left working. The combination of written working and verbal protocol in the penultimate example is very revealing and shows exactly how the pupil's subtraction procedure works when he works left to right and attempts to borrow and pay back. The correctness, sequence and speed of the last example is also very revealing, and shows a case in which the pupil successfully treats a subtraction as a complementary addition.

So when we replay a tape we can distingusih the sequence of operations carried out by the pupil, including whether the working is left to right, right to left, or some combination. We can obtain timing informaion on each individual step and we can detect from the verbal protocol when the pupil consders and then rejects a problem solving step. The Cyclops recording apparatus is ideal for longtitudinal studies because it is easy to operate by teachers and pupils and because audio tapes are a cheap recording medium. The visual quality of data is excellent and some has already been adapted for Open University television programmes for the course 'Developing Mathematical Thinking'.

5. Understanding children's learning strategies

So far we have focussed on collecting data and modelling the execution of particular arithmetic tasks. However we should examine how children learn problem solving skills and also examine the variation in how children organise their own learning. This information will help us to model changes in skill.

A pilot study was carried out using an Open University package called CICERO which facilitates the preparation of computer-administered tutorials as part of the teaching course. This was used to construct tutorials in elementary word problems for nine to twelve year old pupils. Forty-two tutorials on different, though interrelated, aspects of these were implemented, and a computer terminal was installed in a primary school for six months. The relationships between the tutorials were set out in a chart, and each pupil was free to explore his chart in whatever way he preferred. Each pupil was told that the ultimate goal was to be able to tackle a set of miscellaneous problems but that he could choose whatever route he wanted. He had to decide for himself the combination and sequence of subgoals on which he would work, that is, he chose both the tutorials he would study and the order in which he would tackle them.

Altogether 47 pupils, all the nine, ten, eleven and twelve year olds in a village primary school, worked with this system. On average each pupil spent six sessions of approximately half an hour working on his own at the terminal, in total attempting some fifteen tutorials. In that time 25 pupils actually 'finished' that is they successfully completed the ultimate goal, tutorial 42, the miscellaneous set of problems. Six more children were well on the way to completion.

In analysing and attempting to provide parsimonious descriptions of the 47 different sequences of tutorials and the associated reasons for choosing each one, it proved useful to look at two aspects. One was the degree to which an individual pupil sought some kind of overview of the material, and the other the degree to which he could cope with local contingencies. Put another way, the first aspect refers to the learner's wish to see the general shape of the wood despite the trees, and the second to his ability to cope with the obstacles that individual trees present. Such aspects are respectively akin to the descriptions of comprehension learning and operation learning that Pask has used in analysing adult learning strategies [12].

In this case, comprehension learning could happen in one of three ways:
   a) by asking the experimenter questions about the chart and the subject matter it represented (the experimenter was always present)
   b) by consulting summary cards which outlined each tutorial
   c) by exploring tutorials.

The children fell into three clear categories in this respect:
   i) low comprehension learning: virtually no attempt to gain any kind of overall picture (26 pupils).
   ii) average comprehension learning: enough done to enable the child to see one clear route to the top of the chart from wherever he considered himself to be, this information usually gleaned by asking questions and/or consulting cards, i.e. methods (a) and (b) above. (9 pupils).
   iii) high comprehension learning: enough explanation done to enable the child to see multiple routes and to have a relatively full grasp of what is involved, this information obtained by using all three methods (a), (b) and (c) (12 pupils).

With respect to operation learning, that is the degree of local organisation they manifested, the children could be allocated to four fairly clear categories, each of which more or less subsumes its predecessor. These categories were:
   i) low operation learning: random dotting about with no

coherent stratgegy ever emerging. (3 pupils)

ii) below average operation learning: an ability to
   respond to local contingencies, for example when
   unsuccessful. A child in this category would take
   appropriate action, either repeating the tutorial,
   opting for a relevant prerequisite, or tackling an
   analagous one. (13 children)

iii) above average operation learning: the ability of
   category (ii) above plus an ability to plan short
   sequences of tutorials, and adhere to these. (10
   pupils)

iv) high operation learning: the abilities of (ii) and
   (iii) plus an ability to plan well ahead on at least
   one occasion. (21 pupils)

Our conclusion from the experiment [5] is that pupils can
achieve a reasonably high level of operation learning
without having any sense of the way their learning fits into
a broader pattern. Results like this are clearly important
if we are to study how pupils learn arithmetic. So the
combination of experiments and open computer-administered
learning environment could be used to detect variation in
the pupil's learning strategy.

6. Recording children's learning strategies

We are in the process of re-implementing Floyd's chart
system on a Terak microcomputer using the Edinburgh
University LOGO software [15]. It is easy to implement these
charts on a display.

Each of the rectangle represents a computer tutorial, and
the number included in each is just a label for that
tutorial so that for example if a pupil wishes to take the
tutorial on volume sums, he asks for tutorial 31. The oval
beneath each tutorial indicates the direct prerequisites for
that tutorial. In order to be in a position to attempt
tutorial 40, WEIGHT PROBLEMS, for instance, it is necessary
to know something about weight and its measurement (W), to
be able to do elementary computations in decimal arithmetic
(D), and to be able to determine just what computation is
necessary to solve word problems involving weight (WS). The
circle above each tutorial contains what the system
considers a pupil to have learned if he completes a tutorial
successfully. Thus the P above tutorial 40 indicates that
the successful student has achieved some skill in word
problem-solving.

Pupils are allowed to opt for any tutorial on any occasion
provided that one of the following classes of reason can be
given:

a) all the necessary direct prerequisites already

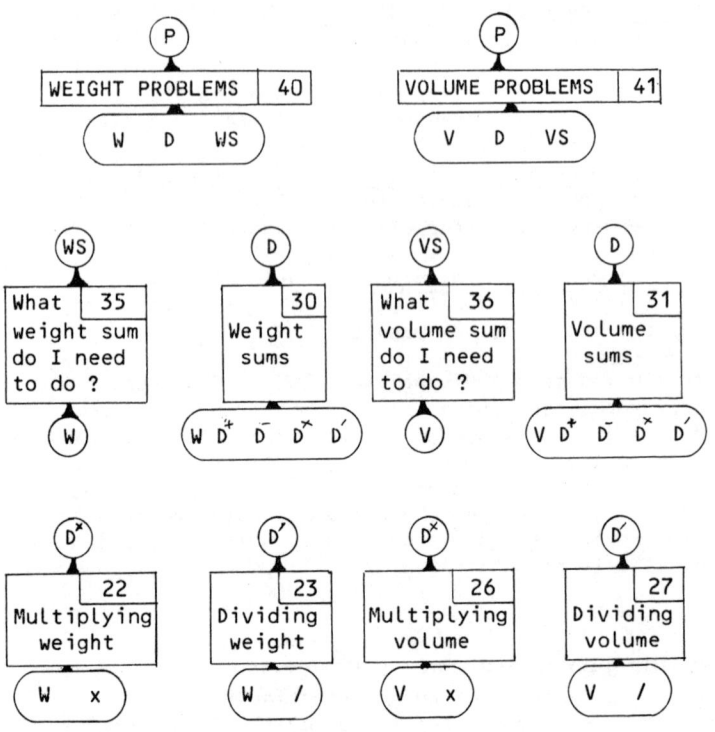

Fig. 3   An example chart

obtained.
b) an analogous tutorial already successfully completed.
c) a desire to explore what is involved, with a
reasonable chance of success.

A type (a) reason for attempting tutorial 40 would be that
prerequisites W, D and WS had already been obtained by
successful completion of previous tutorials. A type (b)
reason for the same tutorial would be that tutorial 41 had
been successfully completed. That is, a pupil having met
with success in doing volume problems would be allowed to
attempt weight problems because in a certain sense the two
classes of problems are analogous. A legitimate type (c)
reason for this same tutorial would be a stated desire to
see just what these problems were like, expressed by a child
who could not give reasons (a) and (b) but who had not
previously failed at any lower level tutorial.

In addition to the considerable range of options that these three types of reason give to the pupil, there is the flexibility afforded by the essential redundancy of the chart, so that it is not remotely necessary to study all the tutorials before attempting the final one. There are several instances of redundancy in Figure 2. For example the subgoal D (decimal arithmetic) can be obtained by succesfuly completing tutorial 30 or 31: it is not necessary to do both. In the complete chart there are three other tutorials whose end-product is also subgoal D.

These charts and their interfaces are easy to implement in Edinburgh LOGO. Each pupil has a disk of his own with his charts left in the state they were when last used by him. The LOGO software provides an automatic dribble facility so that when the experimenter removes a pupil's disk from the classroom he can retrieve a complete record of the pupil's interactions including timing information. Also by embedding the chart system in LOGO it is possible for pupils to carry out mathematical experiments in that language [7]. Further we can augment the chart system with a student model and teaching rules [11] so that different teaching interactions can be experimented with.

7. Conclusion

Currently the modelling tools available for studies of children's mathematical learning have an expressive power that does not match the low quality of the data of pupils' mathematical working available. The two main sources of data currently used are large collections of scripts taken at individual points of time and longtitudinal records of individual pupil's mathematical development taken by individual teachers.

We have developed two microcomputer based systems which can be used unobtrusively in classrooms without experimenter intervention and provide low cost data storage. They will allow us to answer questions like
  i) In a particular two column subtraction sum, did the pupil cross out or decrement first?
  ii) How long did the pupil pause at the critical step, and did the pupil say to herself 'five from three makes two' before completing the sum?
  iii) How did the pupil sketch the problem?
  iv) At what point in the year did the pupil decide she had mastered a certain skill?
  v) What strategies did she use to achieve and establish skill mastery?

We believe that this application of microcomputer technology will yield high quality longtitudinal data. This will be applied to improve the existing computational models of mathematical competence. Another of our longterm objectives is to improve these sufficiently to permit their incorporation as student models [16] in intelligent mathematics computer tutors. Such models can be used to train teachers in mathematical diagnosis. For example Brown and Burton [3] have employed their subtraction models in a computer program which mimics the various subtraction strategies for trainee teachers who give the program subtractionn problems to do. Similarly models of mathematical competence can be used to develop and refine highly diagnostic tests for use in the classroom. One of our longterm objectives is to design open based learning environments which support pupils in planning and organising their mathematical development.

Acknowledgements

The research described in this chapter is being carried out in collaboration with Richard Young. We are indebted to Jim Howe for comments on a draft of the chapter and for providing us with access to the Edinburgh LOGO system and Graham Read for prompting our use of Cyclops. Peter Ross, Ken Johnson, Mark I'Anson and Dave Liddell have given us invaluable technical help.

References

1. R.B.ASHLOCK, Error Patterns in Computation, Bell and Howell, 1976.

2. M.BENNET, SUBSTITUTOR: A teaching program. Unpublished project report, Department of Artificial Intelligence, University of Edinburgh, 1976.

3. J.S.BROWN and R.R.BURTON, Diagnostic models for procedural bugs in basic mathematical skills, Cognitive Science, 2, pp. 155-192, 1978.

4. J.S.BROWN and K.VANLEHN, Repair Theory: A generative theory of bugs in procedural skills, Cognitive Science, 4, 1980.

5. A.FLOYD, Children's stratgegies in a computer-assisted learning environment, Open University CAL Tech. Report, 1981.

6. H.GINSBURG, How children Learn Arithmetic, Van Nostrand, 1977.

7. J.A.M.HOWE, T. O'SHEA and F.PLANE, Learning Mathematics through LOGO programming, in Computer Assisted Learning - Scope Programs and Limits, Tagg and Lewis, North Holland, 1980.

8. D.KLAHR and J.G.WALLACE, Cognitive development: An information processing view, Erlbaum, 1976.

9. F.G.LANKFORD, Some computational strategies of seventh grade pupils, ERIC Reports, School of Education, Virginia University, 1972.

10. A.NEWELL and H.A.SIMON, Human Problem Solving, Prentice-Hall, 1972.

11. T.O'SHEA, A self-improving quadratic tutor, Int. Journal Man Machine Studies, 11, pp. 97-124, 1979.

12. G.PASK, Style and strategies of learning, Br. Journal Ed. Psychol., 46, pp. 128-148, 1976.

13. G.READ, An application of microcomputing to teaching at a distance, Education Broadcasting International, June 1977.

14. L.B.RESNICK (ed.), Hierarchies in children's learning: a symposium, Instructional Science, 2, pp. 311-362, 1973.

15. P.M.ROSS, TERAK LOGO User's Manual, Department of Artificial Intelligence Occasional Paper no. 21, Edinburgh University, 1980.

16. J.A.SELF, Student models in CAI, Int. Journal Man Machine Studies, 6, pp. 261-276, 1974.

17. P.WOODS and J.R.HARTLEY, Some learning models for arithmetic tasks and their use in computer-based learning, Br. Journal Ed. Psychol., 41, pp. 39-48, 1971.

18. R.M.YOUNG, Seriation by children: an artificial intelligence analysis of a Piagetian task, Basel: Birkhauser, 1976.

19. R.M.YOUNG and T.O'SHEA, Errors in children's subtraction, appearing in Cognitive Science.

MICROCOMPUTERS
AND CREATIVE WRITING

Mike Sharples

The Open University

1. Introduction

There are few examples of computer aids for education in
language arts and, of those few, most provide pupils with
drill and practice exercises in grammar, spelling or writing
style. The computer programs described below are different.
They offer powerful and general learning aids - a sentence
generator, a story planner, a word processor/text
transformer, an automated thesaurus and dictionary, a
spelling corrector - which may be used both by the teacher
to demonstrate language construction and by the pupil to
compose and alter text. Being tools rather than teaching
systems they are not aligned to a particular syllabus and,
as the linguistic information is held in simple data files,
the programs may be easily modified to manipulate other
languages - from Latin to mathematical expressions. The
paper begins with a brief history and critique of computer
assisted instruction (CAI) followed by an impression of a
computer-based 'Workshop' for exploring language and
creative writing and, lastly, an account of a project with
eleven year old children who used a prototype part of the
workshop in a creative writing course.

2. Background

In the mid 1960's CAI was heralded as 'one way of injecting
interest, excitement and efficiency into education' [5].
Teaching machines would take over the burden of rote
teaching, provide lessons designed and paced for each pupil
and offer detailed information on esoteric subjects. The
human teacher would be promoted to classroom manager,
responsible for planning a syllabus, preparing course work
and tending a flock of teaching machines.

> "For so long teaching has been regarded as a human task
> that it is novel to suggest a machine should take over
> the role of contact with students, and leave a teacher
> to do the planning and preparation of the lesson. But it
> does seem to work, and in a world that is short of
> teachers there is every reason to develop it as far as
> possible." [5]

Fifteen years later little has apparently changed. CAI never swept through the education system, but the optimism has returned and with it the claims and predictions, transferred to a new generation of computers. The instruments may be different, but the tune remains the same, so it is worthwhile examining the problems encountered by designers of education software over the last fifteen years.

To date, CAI, whether from sequential 'frames' of information, or a complex algorithm providing remedial guidance and supplementary exercises, has used teaching material drawn from a fixed set of facts and structured to foresee the demands of the pupils. This prohibits effective computer teaching of subjects that demand up-to-date information, such as current affairs and politics, or a sharing of knowledge and opinions - creative writing is an obvious example. No automated teaching system has been designed that can assimilate loosely stated information, and a current affairs course without current facts, or a creative writing scheme that ignores ideas from the pupils, would be dreary and mildewed.

Furthermore, a skilled teacher alters the course material to suit the local needs and problems of pupils: an extra example to illustrate a concept giving general difficulty; remedial help for the slow learners; project work for the more able. Without similar skills the computer becomes a costly textbook, offering pre-digested facts in an inflexible format.

Thus to be an effective teacher, a CAI system must build up, or be given
  a) a representation of the conceptual framework of the subject to be taught
  b) a representation of the pupils' knowledge in the subject area.
  c) a strategy for identifying concepts which each pupil finds difficult to grasp and thus generating or providing remedial help.

An alternative strategy would be to let the pupil interrogate the computer to gain extra information. This still requires a) and b) plus
  d) a means of communication which allows the pupil to explore the machine's representation of the subject knowledge.

The need for such 'intelligent computer-aided instruction' (ICAI) has occupied researchers for over a decade and two paradigm solutions are O'Shea's Quadratic Tutor [6] and Brown, Burton & Zdybel's Meteorology System [1]. The quadratic tutor generates tutorial problems and, from each pupil's responses, builds up a profile of the pupil, which the program consults to amend its teaching strategy. The meteorology system contains an explicit representation of its subject knowledge and the student learns by interrogating and exploring this through a natural language dialogue with the computer. The limitation of these systems, both the results of extended research projects, lies in the scope of their knowledge. O'Shea's program is confined to teaching about quadratic equations by the 'discovery method', whereas the Brown et al. system only understands and tutors about introductory meteorology. To extend either to another subject area, say differential calculus instead of quadratic equations and geology instead of meteorology, would require the rewriting, by a skilled programmer, of a large part of the program.

A significant advance in ICAI will be the design of systems that permit knowledge and a teaching scheme for a particlar subject to be added as data by a teacher with no programming skills. It is an exciting prospect, not least because it will encourage educators to think deeply about the purpose, content and structure of teaching. If the daunting technical and epistemological problems can be overcome (for instance, the sizable computer memory required and the difficulties of representing large amounts of organised knowledge) there still remain the educational issues of curriculum design and teaching strategy: should a computer-based economics tutor contain knowledge about a Keynsian economic system, a Marxist one, a monetarist one, or a blend of all three? And what of an English language ICAI system, given as many prescriptions for literary style as there are authors?

For computer-aided language teaching, a conservative approach would be to restrict the teaching material to an accepted core of 'correct' language concepts, such as simple grammar and formal styles, but this is no more than a reappearance, in the guise of modern technology, of the old prescriptive grammar lessons, now widely criticised as being irrelevant, or even harmful, to a child's language development.

Designers and users of CAI programs are already being lured by technology and the constraints of the curriculum into accepting inferior teacher substitutes, equipped with outmoded and incomplete principles of education. No headmaster would welcome a teacher with a didactic and patronising style, knowledge confined to a single teaching scheme and poor ability to meet the wide range of demands from pupils; market it as a 'microcomputer teaching package' and every school wants one. The alternative is to leave out the teaching component and instead use the computer as a 'learning aid', to solve problems, perform or simulate experiments and access information. It is familiar ground – computers are generally used for academic research in one of these three roles – but the task for educationalists is to design programming languages, simulation packages and databases for use by people with no knowledge of computer-programming. These would have the advantages – flexibility, generality, power – over CAI of any resource (say a paint box and blank paper) over a teaching kit (say a painting-by-numbers set) and also the problems, including lack of constraint and direction.

What follows is not, therefore, a plea to abandon computer-assisted instruction, but rather to subject it to the same audit as human teaching (with a good 'author language' it takes around 100 hours to prepare and program one hour of conventional CAI teaching material) and to suit it to the best prevailing educational principles. A CAI package may well be suited to the teaching of simple arithmetic, or introductory computer programming; it is certainly not the best aid for creative writing and language understanding.

3. Computer-based language education

English language teaching in Britain is in turmoil. Neither prescriptive Latinate grammar, nor the study of English literature has been found to offer much help to a child struggling to write coherent and fluent essays yet the findings of contemporary research in psychology and linguistics have not been widely applied to teaching. They suggest that if a child is to develop her writing in a controlled manner she must learn to plan a story form, to create text suited to audience and function and to understand and manipulate the structures of language. An exceptional scheme, which incorporates these ideas is 'Language in Use' [4]. Based on modern descriptive linguistics, 'Language in Use' encourages the pupil to explore the structure of language by, for example. playing with word order, writing advertising copy or inventing nonsense words. The pupil's linguistic knowledge is applied to creative writing through controlled composition exercises.

Useful and invigorating though it is, 'Language in Use' has never gained wide acceptance in the classroom, partly because it is a broad teacher's guide rather than a detailed text and partly due to a lack of aids for language exploration. Until now there have been no facilities for children to easily generate sentences from a grammar; add syntactic and semantic constraints; discover the effects of simple transformational rules; explore alternative story styles; quickly access composing aids, such as a thesaurus. Natural language computer programs can offer just such a expose a child's intuitive knowledge of language and, by addressing issues of style rather than correctness, use it to extend his skills of creative writing.

4. Language workshop

The language workshop which will be described below, loosely
based on the 'Language in Use' teaching scheme, has the same
general function and components as a carpentry workshop: a
set of tools, to explore, construct and modify text; a
stockpile of useful linguistic parts such as definitions and
synonyms; a detailed instruction manual describing the
function of each tool and a 'Teach Yourself' Guide
suggesting games, exercises and projects in story building.

The Guide begins by introducing a series of generative
grammars which lead the child into an exploration of the
structure and function of language. By specifying first an
appropriate vocabulary, then syntactic structure and then
meaning the child can use the computer to generate
interesting and increasingly refined stories and poems.

4.1 GRAM1
GRAM1 is a random word generator which allows the child to
place words in a vocabulary and then, by selecting words at
random, generate unordered strings of words. Each grammar is
described and simulated using paper slips so, for GRAM1, one
word is written on each slip of paper which is then placed
in a 'vocabulary box'. The slips are drawn out blindfold and
the words copied onto paper.

The child then carries out the same process with the
computer, using simple commands (PUT, GET, CLEAR) and guided
by prompts (the W: prompt signifies the computer is waiting
for a command). The child's responses in the following
dialogue are underlined, and comments are enclosed in angle
brackets:

> W: put <add words to the vocabulary>
> WORDS: the a song sunset fades man woman slowly sad
> W: get <generate word strings>
> NUMBER OF WORDS IN A LINE: 5
> NUMBER OF LINES: 3
>
> ***
>
> woman sunset song fades a
> sad slowly fades sunset song
> the sad slowly a man
>
> ***

GRAM1 accustoms the child to using a computer, provides
simple metaphors for linguistic terms (for example
'vocabulary' is 'the box that holds words') and demonstrates
that language consists of more than a random string of
words. Through choosing words on a single theme the child
also starts to build functional vocabularies which she will
use later to develop her creative writings.

4.2 GRAM 2

Exercises and games in the Guide prompt the child to think
about the order of words in a sentence and lead her on to a
grammar with syntactic constraints - GRAM2. First the word
slips in the vocabulary box are sorted into new boxes
according to part of speech. The Guide then provides
templates for 'silly stories' which must be completed by
choosing, at random, words of the appropriate part of
speech:

> Template: The adjective noun eats the noun adverb with a
> noun.

> Completed story: The tiny bicycle eats the wall sometimes
> with a peanut.

The next step is for the child to form her own story
templates, initially by substituting single parts of speech
and later by writing regularly occurring patterns such as:
'ARTICLE ADJECTIVE NOUN' or 'ARTICLE NOUN is ADJECTIVE'. The
GRAM2 computer program makes the whole process of generating
the sentences faster and more exciting:

> W: put <add generation rules>
> PART OF SPEECH: name <part of speech>
> WORDS: Thatcher\Sproggs\Reagan\Muldoon
>   <words generated from parts of speech, alternatives
>   are separated by backslash '\'>
>
> PART OF SPEECH: noun
> WORDS: igloo\telephone\bicycle\lampshade\cat\banana
>
> PART OF SPEECH: noun
> WORDS: looked\walked\roller-skated\pushed
>
> PART OF SPEECH: adverb
> WORDS: sadly\stupidly\grandly\overwhelmingly\nastily
>
> PART OF SPEECH: adjective
> WORDS: bold\sad\dangerous\wise\stupid\round\square
>
> PART OF SPEECH:

PUT FINISHED

```
W: get <generate from story pattern>
PATTERN: One day Mrs. name verb out of her noun
PATTERN: and shouted "noun!",adverb,to a adjective
PATTERN: noun near her noun.
PATTERN:
```

****

One day Mrs. Sproggs roller-skated out of her
Lampshade and shouted "Igloos!"stupidly to a
dangerous banana near her cat.

****

GET FINISHED

The text now begins to look more like English, but it still
lacks a vital ingredient - agreement of meaning. Using GRAM3
the child can select the words and phrases that should be
matched for meaning.

```
W: put
PART OF SPEECH: adjective <add parts of speech, with
                          associated words and meanings to
                          vocabulary>
WORDS: fierce\tame\furry
MEANING: animal

PART OF SPEECH: adjective
WORDS: tiny\small\little
MEANING: small

PART OF SPEECH: adjective
WORDS: huge\enormous\large
MEANING: big

PART OF SPEECH: adjective
WORDS: stupid\silly\fat\thin
MEANING: human

PART OF SPEECH: noun
WORDS: giant
MEANING: human big

PART OF SPEECH: noun
WORDS: rat\mouse\frog
MEANING: animal small

PART OF SPEECH: noun
WORDS: whale\elephant
MEANING: animal big
```

144

```
PART OF SPEECH:

PUT FINISHED

W: get <generate from pattern>

PATTERN: Once there was a adjective 1 noun 1
PATTERN: that lived with a adjective 2
PATTERN: adjective 3 noun 2 3.
PATTERN:


***************************************************

Once there was a tiny frog that lived with
a huge stupid giant.

***************************************************

GET FINISHED
```

A number following a part of speech indicates that it is to
be matched for meaning with another, similarly numbered,
part of speech. Rules may be stored in a computer file and
then recalled at a later session. The computer is now an
essential aid - without it word selection would be difficult
and tedious. The child has gained access to a powerful
linguistic tool, a context-free grammar with semantic
constraints, and in the process learned to describe and
manipulate language. Such skills are a necessary
prerequisite for the second stage of the course, in which
the child's linguistic knowledge is applied to creative
writing.

The Guide now describes the remaining tools in the language
workshop. They are of three types: composing aids, reference
aids and diagnostic aids.

5. Composing aids

According to modern linguistics [2] creative writing is a
three stage process comprising: idea formation, text
production and text revision. Thus a writer first produces a
complex mental network of ideas, plots and story segments.
This 'story plan' is then turned into a visible text, which
is finally revised and polished. A clear awareness of the
process, and of the constraints imposed at each stage, can
help an author to plan a well-structured story or overcome
such hazards as 'cold start' (the problem of knowing where
and how to begin a composition) and 'writer's block' (being
unable to express ideas as text). The workshop's composing
aids are designed to clarify and assist each stage of
composition.

5.1 PLAN

Using the PLAN program a pupil builds and explores a
story plan by creating structured story elements. At each
stage the program suggests alternative ways to expand or
decode the plan. The user may choose to construct a simple
linear narrative, or a highly embellished descriptive
passage. Here PLAN is being used to describe a house. The
diagrams show the story elements constructed at each stage
and, by arrows, the possible ways to expand them. The
heavily outlined titles indicate the current position in the
story plan:

```
W: story

NAME OF STORY: house

    *********************
          HOUSE
    *********************
```

```
    CHOICES
    1. WRITE HOUSE
    2. FINISH

    CHOICE: 1

        STORY - HOUSE

    HOUSE: kitchen

    ***********************
          KITCHEN
    ***********************
```

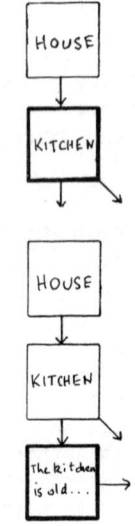

```
    CHOICES
    1. WRITE KITCHEN
    2. MAKE A NEW PART OF HOUSE
    3. FINISH

    CHOICE: 1

        STORY - HOUSE - KITCHEN

    KITCHEN: The kitchen is old and damp
    KITCHEN: and smells of garlic.
    KITCHEN:

    CHOICES
    1. WRITE SOME MORE
    2. MAKE A NEW PART OF KITCHEN
    3. LOOK AT HOUSE
    4. FINISH
```

146

CHOICE: 2

    STORY — HOUSE — KITCHEN

KITCHEN: In the corner is a high shelf
KITCHEN:

CHOICES
1. WRITE SOME MORE
2. SHOW 'The kitchen is old...'
3. MAKE A NEW PART OF KITCHEN
4. LOOK AT HOUSE
5. FINISH

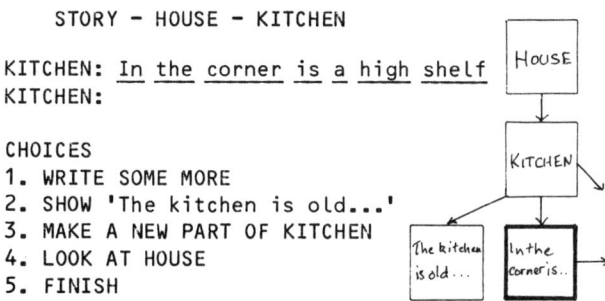

CHOICE: 1

    STORY — HOUSE — KITCHEN
    In the corner is a high shelf.

MORE: shelf

****
       SHELF
****

CHOICES
1. WRITE SHELF
2. SHOW 'The kitchen is old...'
3. MAKE A NEW PART OF KITCHEN
4. LOOK AT HOUSE
5. FINISH

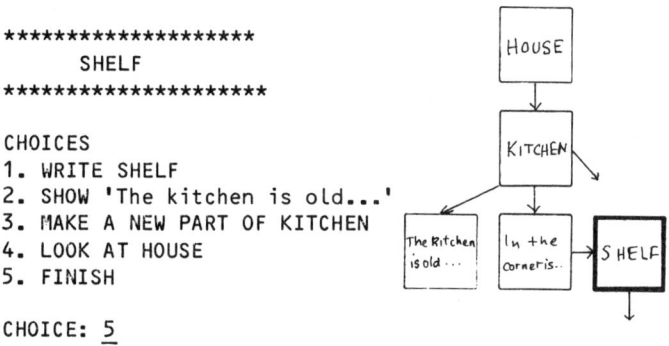

CHOICE: 5

    HOUSE STORY FINISHED

The story plan can now be explored: As each story element is
reached its text is both typed out by the computer's printer
and saved on a memory file. Thus the series of short
sentences can later be linked and revised.

    W: show

    NAME OF STORY: house

    STORY — HOUSE

    CHOICES
    1. KITCHEN
    2. FINISH

    CHOICE: 1

```
          STORY - HOUSE - KITCHEN

     CHOICES
     1. 'The kitchen is old...'
     2. 'In the corner is...'
     3. LOOK AT THE REST OF HOUSE
     4. FINISH

     CHOICE: 1

          STORY - HOUSE - KITCHEN
          The kitchen is old and damp and
          smells of garlic.

     CHOICES
     1. 'In the corner is...'
     2. LOOK AT THE REST OF HOUSE
     3. FINISH

     CHOICE: 1

          STORY - HOUSE - KITCHEN
          In the corner is a high shelf.

     CHOICES
     1. SHELF
     2. 'The kitchen is old...
     3. LOOK AT THE REST OF HOUSE
     4. FINISH

     CHOICE: 4

          HOUSE STORY SHOWN

     W:
```

Exercises in the Guide use PLAN to explain function
categories (the differences, for example, between narrative,
descriptive and instructional writing) and to describe
writing styles.

5.2 TRAN

Once the framework of a story has been built using PLAN,
another program, TRAN, may be used to revise the text.
Using TRAN the child can type text to the computer, or recall
it from a memory file, alter it using either simple editing
commands (for word substitution, spelling correction etc.)
or more sophisticated grammatical transformations and then
print out the final version. The transformations are invoked
by rules which can either be written by the child or, more

commonly, retrieved from a computer 'library file'. One rule
allows the child to delete selected parts of speech, another
to explore the effect of sentence combining using relative
clauses. Below is an annotated TRAN session.

```
W: new <type in a new story to TRAN>

STORY: Once there was a pretty princess. The princess
STORY: lived in a big house in a forest. The forest
STORY: was drak. She was very lonely because she had
STORY: no friends to play with.
STORY:

NEW FINISHED

W: change <alter text>

OLD WORDS: drak
NEW WORDS: dark <correct spelling>

OLD WORDS: house
NEW WORDS: castle <substitute words>

OLD WORDS:

**************************************************

Once there was a pretty princess. The princess
lived in a big castle in a forest. The forest was
dark. She was very lonely because she had no
friends to play with.

**************************************************
CHANGE FINISHED

W: lookup <look up computer file to associate a
            part of speech with each word>

LOOKUP FINISHED

W: try <see effect of change but don't
        permanently alter text>
OLD WORDS: noun1 WORDS1 noun2 <swop pairs of
                               nouns in a sentence>
NEW WORDS: noun2 WORDS noun1 <a number appended to
                            'WORDS' matches any text>
OLD WORDS:
```

```
**************************************************

Once there was a pretty princess. The castle lived
in a big princess in a forest. The forest was dark.
She was very lonely because she had no friends to
play with.

**************************************************

W: change

OLD WORDS:      <Press 'return key' after 'OLD WORDS'
                        for 'RULES' prompt>
RULES: combine <use a prewritten rule for sentence
                                combining>

**************************************************

Once there was a pretty princess who lived in a big
castle in a dark forest. She was very lonely
because she had no friends to play with.

**************************************************

W: print
```

"Combine" applies three transformation rules: a 'reduced
relative' rule (to produce 'Once there was a pretty
princess. The princess lived in a big castle in a dark
forest.'); a 'relative rule' (to produce 'Once there was a
pretty princess which lived in a big castle in a dark
forest.') and a 'who' rule (to produce the final transformed
sentence). The 'print' command causes the computer to print
out the final version of the story. With a text editor,
such as TRAN, paragraphs or pages can be quickly added,
deleted and swopped. Thus the child can focus on the parts
needing revision, rather than laboriously copying and
recopying the entire text. Naturally the child must first
learn to recognise the sections needing revision and, for
this, the Guide offers exercises using TRAN. For example
children's essays are often vague, clouded by words such as
'the thing', 'someone' or 'a bit'. Rather than attempting to
correct all these idiosyncracies of style TRAN lets the
child realise the effect of imprecision by presenting a rule
which takes it to the extreme:

```
W: new

STORY: Once there was a pretty princess who lived
STORY: in a big castle in a dark forest. She was
STORY: very lonely because she had no friends to
STORY: play with.
STORY:
```

NEW FINISHED

W: <u>try</u>

OLD WORDS:

RULES: <u>thing</u>

****

Once there was someone pretty who lived in
something big in something else which is dark. She
was very lonely because she had no people to play
with.

****

5.3 Reference Aids
A dictionary and a thesaurus are complicated for a child to
use in book form. The language workshop introduces them as
quick and painless writing aids:

    W: <u>new</u>
    STORY: <u>Once there was</u>
    STORY: <interrupt story by pressing "thesaurus"
           button on keyboard>

****

Word to be looked up: <u>pretty</u>

pretty(adjective): beautiful,elegant,lovely,
                   attractive
pretty(adverb): fairly,rather,somewhat

****

STORY: <u>an elegant princess</u>... <resume typing story>

5.4 Diagnostic Aids
Spelling is one area of writing in which there is general
agreement over correctness. The workshop contains a spelling
correction and diagnosis program which can be used to
monitor the text as it is being typed, or can be applied to
a written story stored in a computer file. The program
contains a simple parser which recognises some correctly
spelt words that are used wrongly in context ('their' in the

phrase 'Once their' in the example below).

STORY: Once their was a pretty princess who

****

SPELLING CHECK: Once THEIR was a PRETTY PRINCESS who
                    <spelling monitor interrupts
                    typing of story>
THEIR means 'belonging to them'. Should the word be
THERE meaning 'in that place'? Yes

Should PRETTY be PRETTY meaning 'beautiful'? Yes

Alter the story by typing the correct words:

****

STORY: Once there was a pretty princess who...
            <computer types out story so far, apart
            from words missplelt>
STORY: lived all alone......

The program also produces a diagnosis of the type of errors
made, which can later be consulted by the child or teacher.
For example it might group 'prety' and 'speling' as 'double
letter errors'.

6. Language workshop—the truth

The language workshop as described above does not exist,
nor has the Guide been written. It is more than a wild
fantasy though – the GRAM1-3 and TRAN programs, exactly as
described, have been written in the POP2 language and
implemented on a PDP 11/60 computer. The thesaurus and
dictionary reference programs are available and should soon
be sold as standard commercial software for home computers.
PLAN has not yet been implemented, but is a logical
extension of a Storymaker program, used in education
research at Bolt Beranek and Newman [3] and is similar in
structure to the Fantasy game described below. It uses a
standard 'tree search' algorithm. Spelling error detection
and correction programs already exist and a spelling
diagnosis program, similar to the one described above, will
be one outcome of a current research project [7]. The
problems lie not in designing and implementing the computer
programs, but in integrating them into a useful and
presentable learning resource.

The first steps have already been taken. In a pilot project,
six pupils (average age 11 years 7 months) of an Edinburgh
school visited Edinburgh University for 2-4 hours a week

over 2 school terms to use a computer-based creative
writing course. They worked from written worksheets which
presented games, exercises, questions and instructions for
the use of the computer. The course was in two sections. In
the first part the children developed their understanding
and manipulation of language. They played word games such as
a sentence construction version of SCRABBLE, and used the
GRAM programs to create sentences and poems. This gave the
children a foundation for the second part of the course in
which they explored and improved their written style. The
next section below describes, in detail, a series of
worksheets from the second part of the course, concerned
with descriptive writing.

7. Descriptive writing

The children began the section by playing language games
designed to expand their range of descriptive words and
phrases. One game made use of rules for the GRAM2 program
which substituted an asterisk for an adjective and an
exclamation mark for an adverb. As the computer only
recognised some 200 words, the purpose of the game was to
'outwit' the machine by inventing sentences with unusual
modifiers, which would not be substituted by the program.
The pupils were provided with core sentences, which they
then embellished, for example 'The man sat on the bench'.

W: get

PATTERN: The old grey-haired man sat sadly on
PATTERN: the uneven green bench.
PATTERN:

++*********A A A********************************

The * grey-haired man sat ! on the uneven * bench.

****

To break the childen from their normal clutch of uninspired
modifiers - 'big', 'nasty', 'horrible' etc. - an on-line
thesaurus provided them with up to eight synonyms of a
common word.

W: thesaurus
WORD TO BE LOOKED UP: big

    big: large,huge,gigantic,giant,massive,important

The children were then introduced to the constraints and
conventions of story content, again through games and
exercises. In one game a group of children wrote a

description of an unusual picture; the description was passed to another group who attempted to redraw the picture, guided only by the written description. This proved to be a useful exercise of descriptive completeness - one group's description, for instance, omitted any mention of colour; the second team complained that they could not draw the picture as they had no idea which coloured crayons to use. From the exercises the children formed a strategy and checklist for descriptive composition. They were then encouraged to break down the process of descriptive writing into manageable stages - planning, draft writing, revision - with the aid of a computer-based game. The children were split into two groups. Each group drew up a plan of the rooms of a haunted house and then wrote descriptions of each room, plus details of treasure and the occupants of the house. The descriptions were incorporated into a game, similar to the popular 'Adventure' computer game and the opposing group then 'explored' the house, fought off the inhabitants and found the treasure by typing commands to the program. Below is the start of a game session. The descriptions were written entirely by one group of the children (game commands are underlined).

Welcome to FANTASY

You are in a long straight hallway with brown oak walls, hanging on the walls are old victorian pictures. On the ground is a telephone table and chair.

a wooden door leads south
a front door leads east

<u>south</u>

You are in a blue coloured bedroom, with a mysterious atmosphere there is a strange rattling noise coming from the window. In the bedroom there is a toilet which is at the left hand corner. There is a chest of drawers and a wardrobe to match. In front of the bed there is a grey, wet mist.

a wooden door leads north
a wooden door leads west

a chef has just arrived through a wooden door (west)

<u>objects</u>

you can see
1 - a gold bracelet and earrings to match.
2 - a bottle of wine

The children then discussed their experiences of playing

Fantasy and formed them into a written adventure story using the TRAN program as a simple text editor. The role of the computer game was to aid the children in transforming static descriptions into dynamic narrative and to provide a focus for discussion on alternative methods of story construction.

8. Results

In terms of performance during the entire pilot scheme the children can be divided into 3 pairs. One pair seemed unable to view written text as an object for manipulation and improvement, and they gained little benefit from the first section of the course. Initially they showed no enthusiasm for writing and their early written products were terse and uncoordinated. These children were not taken through the second section, but instead used a computer text processor to compose, modify and print short descriptive pieces. Once they discovered that the computer could aid the tedious process of revision and presentation, their interest in writing increased and they produced articles for a class newsletter and items for the children's page of the local Edinburgh newspaper.

By contrast, two other children showed a strong enthusiasm for language and writing. During the course their ability to manipulate language and revise text improved markedly. One girl in particular, described by her teacher as having "no exposure to books, except through school", developed an interest in language and literature and showed a marked improvement in language understanding and manipulation during classroom English language exercises. Of the two remaining children one, whom the teacher described as "showing no interest in literature, except when forced", completed the course and his later essays showed gleams of imagination. The other, mid way through the course, began to experiment with prose style and, according to her class teacher, "became dramatically addicted to literature during the year and progressed through Enid Blyton to good teenage books."

In summary, the course required some prior ability from the children to view language as an object for experiment and revision. Of the six children, four initially displayed such skills and profited from the opportunity to develop their written style in a conscious and systematic manner. For the two remaining children, the games, exercises and chance to use a computer as a creative tool, revived a flagging interest in creative writing.

The project is now at rest. More work is required to revise the programs and the teaching material and to conduct trials with both children and adults outside the university lab.

9. Conclusion

The GRAM and TRAN programs have already been squeezed onto a Terak personal computer and home computers will soon be available which can hold a complete language workshop.

Given the instruments, who will call the tune? Some home computer manufacturers already offer drill and practise programs in arithmetic or spelling. Programs which teach prescriptive grammar or, with speech output, present spelling lists and dictation exercises, will find a ready market of 'back to basics' English teachers.

A computer-based languge workshop is more troublesome. The pilot project indicated no single method of use - some children tired of the comptuer after five minutes, others worked happily for an hour or more; some preferred to work alone, others used the computer in pairs or groups; some worked smoothly without help, others demanded constant attention and advice. This was expected. The workshop is not intended to replace or relieve the teacher, nor to fit neatly into a school curriculum. It does not offer a structured lesson, nor a well defined and examinable set of facts. It was designed to give a child the experience of a research worker, with control over the content and structure of his learning, tools to carry out worthwhile experiments and equipment to draft and revise the results.

The best location for such a language workshop would be a resource centre, with books and audio-visual material as well as computers, where children can plan their own study and adults would be available as advisors - more like a children's library than a classroom.

The pilot project suggests that children can learn to control and extend their written language in such an environment, and enjoy the experience: for example, two children volunteered to write descriptions of the haunted house rooms as a home exercise and arrived the following week with five pages of imaginatively written text, ready to be added to the computer game.

One interesting application may be special education. Congenitally deaf children, who lack the experience of experimenting and playing with spoken language, have difficulty in interpreting and composing written text. A computer-based language workshop may help them to acquire the vital skills of language manipulation.

The choice between this and computer programs for drill and practise grammar instruction should not be made by computer manufacturers, but by parents, teachers and children.

Acknowledgements

I should like to thank the children of class Primary 7,
South Bridge School, Edinburgh, and their teacher Mrs.
Finlayson for all thier co-operation. I am grateful also to
Dr.Jim Howe and Dr.Ben DuBoulay for their supervision of the
project, to Dr.Peter Ross, Dr. Tim O'Shea and Ms Helen Pain
for comments on the text, and to the SSRC for financial
support.

References

1. J.S.BROWN, R.R.BURTON and F.ZYDBEL, A model-driven
   question answering system for mixed-initiative computer
   assisted instruction, I.E.E.E. Transactions on Systems
   Man and Cybernetics, SMC-3, 1973.

2. B.C.BRUCE, A.COLLINS, A.D.RUBIN and D.G.GENTNER, A
   cognitive science approach to writing, in Writing: the
   Nature Development and Teaching of Written Communication,
   eds. C.H.Frederiksen M.F.Whiteman and J.D.Domonic, 1980.

3. A.RUBIN, Making stories Making sense, Bolt Beranek and
   Newman Inc., Cambridge, Mass., 1980.

4. P.DOUGHTY, J.PEARCE and G.THORNTON, Language in Use,
   Edward Arnold, 1971.

5. H.KAY, B.DODD and M.SIME, Teaching Machines and
   Programmed Instruction, Pelican (out of print).

6. T.O'SHEA, A self-improving quadratic tutor, Int. Journal
   Man-Machine Studies, 11, pp. 97-124, 1979.

7. H.PAIN, A computer aid for spelling error classification
   in remedial teaching, in Proceedings of IFIP 3rd. World
   Conference on Computers in Education, appearing 1981.

LIST OF CONTRIBUTORS

BLANDFORD, C.
Computer-Asisted Teaching Unit, Queen Mary College,
University of London, Mile End Road, London   E7 4NS

du BOULAY, B.
Department of Computing Science, University of
Aberdeen, Old Aberdeen   AB9 2UB

FLOYD, A.
Institute of Educational Technology, The Open
University, Walton Hall, Milton Keynes   MK7 6AA

FRASER, R.
The College of St.Mark and St.John Foundation,
Derriford Road, Plymouth   PL6 8BH

HART, M.L.
Department of Mathematical Sciences,Trent Polytechnic,
Burton Street, Nottingham   NG1 4BU

HARTLEY, R.
Computer Based Learning Project, University of Leeds,
Leeds   LS2 9JT

HOWE, J.A.M.
Department of Artificial Intelligence, University
of Edinburgh, Forrest Hill, Edinburgh   EH1 2QL

JOHNSON, D.C.
Centre for Science Education, Chelsea College,
University of London, Bridges Place, London   SW6 4HR

LEWIS, R.
Computing Group, Chelsea College, University of
London, Polton Place, London   SW6 5PR

O'SHEA, T.
Institute of Educational Technology, The Open
University, Walton Hall, Milton Keynes   MK7 6AA

PANGARO, P.
System Research Developments Ltd., 58 High Street,
Sutton, Surrey   SM1 1EZ

PASK, G.
System Research Developments Ltd., 58 High Street,
Sutton, Surrey SM1 1EZ

ROSS, P.M.
Department of Artificial Intelligence, University of
Edinburgh, Forrest Hill, Edinburgh EH1 2QL

RUSHBY, N.J.
Imperial College Computer Centre, University of
London, Mechanical Engineering Building, Exhibition
Road, London SW7 2BX

SHARPLES, M.
Institute of Educational Technology, The Open
University, Walton Hall, Milton Keynes MK7 6AA

SMITH, P.R.
Computer-Assisted Teaching Unit, Queen Mary College,
University of London, Mile End Road, London E7 4NS

TAGG, W.
Advisory Unit for Computer Based Education, Hertford
County Council, 19 St. Albans Road, Hatfield